50 Years of indian writing

50 Years of indian writing

Golden Jubilee Volume

a commemorative volume highlighting the achievement of post-independence Indian Writing in English and Literature in Translation

edited by

R. K. DHAWAN

The Indian Association for English Studies

Published by
Indian Association for English Studies
J 391, New Rajinder Nagar
New Delhi 110 060

ISBN: 81-7551-067-6

Composed by Pivot Computers, Delhi 110 006
Printed by Chaman Offset, New Delhi 110 002

Contents

Introduction

The Early Fiction

The Recent Fiction

Drama

Poetry

Society and Literature

Contributors

MULK RAJ ANAND is a pioneer of Indian English fiction. He is a prolific writer and has recently published the novel entitled *Nine Moods of Bharata.*

SUMAN BALA teaches at University of Delhi. She has published a book on Joseph Conrad, and several papers on Indian fiction.

INDIRA BHATT, formerly at C.U. Shah Science College, Ahmedabad, is actively engaged in guiding research on Indian fiction.

SUBHASH CHANDRA teaches at University of Delhi. His publications include a book on Thomas Hardy, and several articles on Indian fiction.

BIJAY KUMAR DAS teaches at Ravenshaw College, Cuttack. He has a number of books and articles to his credit.

R.K. DHAWAN teaches at University of Delhi. He has published several books and articles on Commonwealth literature.

V.T. GIRDHARI teaches at People's College, Nanded. He has recently published the book entitled *The Novels of Joseph Conrad.*

NIBIR K. GHOSH teaches at Agra College, Agra. He has recently published the book *Cal culus of Power: Modern American Political Novel.*

S. INDIRA teaches at Dr. L.B. College, Visakhapatnam. Her areas of research include Indian writing and Canadian literature.

PRAFULLA K. JAGADEB teaches at Christ College, Cuttack. His areas of interest include Indian English poetry.

P.S. KASTURE teaches at Akola in Maharashtra. A senior academic, she has several publications to her credit.

S.T. KAPADIA is Professor of Education and Retired Director, School of Phy., Edu. and Phi., Gujarat University.

ALASTAIR NIVEN is Director of Literature, British Council, London. His publications include *D.H. Lawrence, The Writer and His Work* and *The Yoke of Pity: The Fiction of Mulk Raj Anand.*

R. RADHIGA PRIYADHARSHINI teaches at Vellalar College for Women, Erode.

T.J. PURANI teaches English at Smt. S.C.U. Arts College for Girls, Ahmedabad.

K. SUNEETHA RANI teaches at University of Hyderabad. She is engaged in research on Australian aboriginal writing.

SRILATA RAVI teaches at the Department of European Studies at National University of Singapore.

ALKA SAXENA teaches at D.A.V. College, Kanpur. She is a creative writer and a perceptive critic.

A.R. SHUKLA is a senior academic from Gujarat University, Ahmedabad. His areas of interest include Indian English Writing and Canadian literature.

KANNAMAL SRINIVASAN teaches at Vellalar College for Women, Erode. Besides Indian writing, she is interested in American literature.

50 Years of Indian Writing: A Celebration

R.K. DHAWAN

India has contributed significantly to the overall world literature. This contribution of India has been chiefly through the Indian Writing in English, novelists being in the forefront in this respect. A good number of novelists on the contemporary scene have given expression to their creative urge in no other language than English and have brought credit to the Indian English fiction as a distinctive force in the world fiction. To attempt creative expression on a national scale in an alien medium has seldom happened in human history; and it speaks of the prolific quality of the Indian mind to assimilate the newly confronting situations and the complex dilemmas of modern world.

II

In the recent times, a great body of historical fiction has emerged on the literary scene. Many Indian English novelists have turned to the past as much to trace the deepening mood of nationalism as to cherish the memories of the bygone days. A close study of the contemporary novel reveals writers's preoccupation with our historic past and the unabated interest of the readers in the novels that depict the past or that treat some event of national import that has had wide repercussions. As a critic I have always attached a great deal of importance to the impact on a writer of the historical milieu in which he lives and the historical periods of an earlier time with which the author wishes to associate himself by choice. Writers like Khushwant Singh, Manohar Malgonkar, Chaman Nahal, Shashi Tharoor, Salman Rushdie and Amitav Ghosh amply illustrate this point of view.

It is quite improper to compare historical novel with history proper. The novelist concerned with history is beyond the traditional way of assessing events; he has to blend history with his vision and philosophy. The novel deals with history through a camouflage. P.V. Narasimha Rao's maiden novel *The Insider*, for example, is a fictionalized biography of an ex-Prime Minister. Anand, the protagonist of the novel, is an alter-ego of Rao; the major events of his life run parallel to the author's life history. Also, it is an interesting account of the life and times of this country's politics. The loss of idealism and honesty from public life in India, portrayed candidly in the novel, makes a terrific indictment of the system. It is a historical novel that throws useful light on the slice of the country's socio-political life.

An historical novel is nothing but an evaluation of a segment of historical reality as projected by the novelist whose techniques of writing fiction enable him to describe his vision or world-vision. In all his writing, Amitav Ghosh's engagement with history is not the same kind as that of a historian, but this does not in any way lessen its significance as historical fiction. The fictional framework renders history more readable and lively and he is able to involve the reader more than what history does. Ghosh's fiction reveals that the novelist's involvement with history is his prime obsession. Indeed, he interjects a new dimension into his encounter with history. His fiction is imbued with both political and historical consciousness. Ghosh is a novelist who virtually bends his novels to the needs of history; they largely derive their purpose and shape from it.

A distinction must be made here between the conscious use of history and its sub-conscious presentation. The setting of most novels is in the context of some historical framework unless the novelist wilfully places his action in an imaginary locale hoping to highlight a special metaphysical or political point of view, e.g. William Golding's *Lord of the Flies*, George Orwell's *Nineteen Eighty-Four*. Sometimes, he creates the country, as does Joseph Conrad in *Nostromo*. It is my contention that whatever be the perfection of craftsmanship in this type of novel, such works are accepted by the public as nothing more than utopias.

Modern deconstructionists would easily discuss them as exercises in self-deception. Utopias make fine reading; their relevance to the immediate problem is more of an escapist nature suggesting remedies neither available nor practical. The historical novel represents no surface wave of escapism, but a deep, unconscious movement towards national homogeneity. It is in the historical novel only that the actual day-to-day problems of life can be encountered, examined, exposed, challenged and rectified. Entertainment and instruction are, by common consent, most valued virtues of historical fiction. The factual and informational values of history illuminate the subject and increasingly whet the reader's curiosity. In other words, for a true artist history is a hand-maiden which helps him to achieve several purposes. How deft he is in the art of amalgamating the two must be judged only by the finished product. And herein the novelist who makes use of history by choice obviously must be held at a superior level than the one who consciously assimilates it.

A pertinent question that arises is the relevance of history in a work of art. As a matter of fact, historical sense and reality enter into the sphere of art imperceptibly; they are important factors in determining the ultimate value of a given piece of art. In a sense every novelist tries to enshrine a period in a book; in other words every novelist is a historical novelist. This historical reality, in terms of time and space, forms an integral part of a work of art and is transmuted in the process of giving it a creative expression; in the process it achieves wider dimensions of universality and at times a state of timelessness. The historical novelist is none but a historian on whom a talent for imaginative fiction has been happily bestowed.

A writer of historical fiction then is as much a historian as a novelist. But history does impose limitations on him. He is not free to distort history; factual accuracy has to be strictly adhered to. "Herein lies the additional burden," writes Chaman Nahal, "that a historical novelist places on the artist. The novelist is obliged to do careful research into the period he has chosen for presentation and every detail of that period has to be accurate." Detail, not only about the layout of a geographical region, but also about the people living in that region, their mode of speech, their dress, their habits, their peculiar traits and countless other characteristics of that particular community. Indeed every care must be taken to verify incidental details, as a sure guard against anachronism. Before it was published, *Gone with the Wind* was subjected, for a period of eight months, to a rigorous checking of facts; and a systematic verification was made of specific statements contained in the novel. Indeed it is an important reason for the immense popularity of this novel in which Margaret Mitchell makes a serious evocation of the American Civil War.

Again, it is hazardous to infiltrate too much history into the plot of a novel, or to have too many historical figures among the leading characters. History puts the author at a disadvantage since a great majority of characters who have an independent historical reality can hardly be made amenable to the author's designs or the exigencies of the plot. The interaction for historical and fictional characters, and the interaction of the two kinds amongst themselves, is the most challenging part of writing a historical novel.

III

As elsewhere, majority of novels in India have been written in response to historical movements or events such as the Gandhian movement, imperial rule, partition of the country, the emergence of the New India. The heroic effort to throw away the foreign yoke was an epic struggle covering the first half of the twentieth century. The nation was in a ferment; a massive movement for liberation from the foreign rule was raging in the country. The British, who were exploiting India the utmost, were in no mood to withdraw. The struggle was long and gruelling.

The freedom struggle caught the imagination of the entire nation, no less the Indian English writers. No significant writer could escape the impact of the mighty movement sweeping the country. The novels written in the Indian languages and English in the thirties and the forties reflect the vitality of a people devoted to a cause. This is amply reflected in the novels of the period—Raja Rao's *Kanthapura*, Mulk Raj Anand's *Coolie*, K.A. Abbas's *In-*

quilab, D.F. Karaka's *We Never Die* and C.N. Zutshi's *Motherland*.

The novels dealing with the freedom struggle give vivid pictures of the exploitation and the arrogance of the foreign rulers, as also the portrayal of an awakened people struggling for their birthright. The growth of the historical novel coincided with the intensification of the struggle for Indian freedom, especially after the First World War. Novels written previously had confined to religious aestheticism—now the focus shifted to contemporary socio-political concern.

Indeed it were the English who brought with them enlightenment cf the West and inspired the Indians to imbibe the spirit of nationalism. In the early decades of the century, the English system had nearly succeeded in giving the people a unity in law, in public administration, in finance and in education that was hitherto unknown to them and ironically enough all this resulted in generating a sense of national unity which urged them to fight for freedom in later stages.

The intellectuals, be they philosophers, historians or literary artists, have traditionally played significant roles in all national revolutions of the world. Not only do they reach the minds of the people through their writing, they also subject every institution of the society to a specific political philosophy, and through that propagate their point of view.

The Indian English novelists were most responsive to the call of equality, freedom and human rights, for the literary artists have an intrinsic quality and ability to look beyond their time. It is they who hold before the common man a lense, as it were, through which he could see what threatened him socially, culturally or politically, and which made him aware of the precipice that lay ahead. As it was, a number of novels were written during the period that portrayed the unjustness of the British rule and the grim fight the people were determined to give to get rid of it. Politics became synonymous with nationalism.

IV

No doubt, the most important historical event of our age, as is evident from the writings of Indian English novelists, was the partition of the subcontinent. The English in 1947 left the country with bag and baggage, after dividing it into two parts. The religious and political differences between Hindus and Muslims which climaxed with this event led to widespread disturbances, causing destruction of human life on a scale unprecedented in the recent history of the subcontinent. There was let loose a communal fury which caused a great havoc and misery. In the massacres, which immediately preceded the partition and continued for several months afterwards, at least one million Hindus and Muslims lost their lives. There was large-scale migration of people from one country to the other. In the process, thousands were massacred; women were raped, children were flung on spears and property was looted on a vast scale.

The Indian English novelists, like their counterparts in Indian languages, responded to these happenings with a sense of horror. A number of novels were written on the theme of partition, the destruction it brought and the plight of the refugees. They faithfully record the reign of violence that characterized the period and provide a sad, telling commentary on the breakdown of human values. A strain of despair and disillusionment is predominant in these novels. Some significant novels on the theme of partition are Khushwant Singh's *Train to Pakistan*, Chaman Nahal's *Azadi*, Bhisham Sahni's *Tamas*, Shiv K. Kumar's *A River with Three Banks* and Manju Kapur's *Difficult Daughters*.

V

Indian English writers through Salman Rushdie, Vikram Seth, Vikram Chandra, Anita Desai and Arundhati Roy hold centrestage in the contemporary literary scenario. They have received national and international recognition, fabulous royalties and prestigious awards. Amitav Ghosh is perhaps the finest writer among those who were born out of the post-*Midnight's Children* revolution in Indian English fiction.

It was in the year 1993 that the Indian English novel came to be associated with big 'monies.' It started with Vikram Seth's *A Suitable Boy* which was a happy marriage of 'money and imagination.' Seth became India's first millionaire novelist. He was paid a fabulous amount of Rs. 2.5 crores as advance royalty for the novel by the British publishers, Orion. His novel was the high watermark of the Indian literary scene of the early nineties. The novel was short-listed for the Booker Award but could not get it in the final round because the Booker Committee Chairman felt that the novel needed editing. Nonetheless, the novel registered a tremendous sale and fired the imagination of many aspiring fiction writers in the country.

The publication of Arundhati Roy's *The God of Small Things* is the latest and most valuable addition to the corpus of Indian writing. It is pre-eminently a novel by a woman, about a woman, seen through the eyes of a woman. Having received the Booker's Award for the Best Novel of the Year, it is the most talked-about novel in the world today. Indeed it has taken the publishing world by storm. The book has shot the newspaper headlines the worldover, and the media is almost hysterical in highlighting the commercial success of the author. No writer has been paid such a fabulous amount for publishing rights of his/her first novel.

Arundhati Roy is an excellent storyteller, and the novel seems to us a literary sport. We may not hesitate to call it a contemporary classic. It is a modern novel in its theme and the treatment of the theme, a postmodern novel in its knotting and knitting of narrative threads, manipulation of expressive literary forms and creative 'play' with words, a feminist novel in the pity and terror that it evokes for the condition of women in a particular cultural milieu, a political novel in its criticism of the hypocrisy of the communist party, an autobiographical novel in the way the facts of the author's life have been distilled into a verbal artefact and so on. In fact the novel is eminently amenable to multiple approaches and interpretations.

VI

There are several reasons for the popularity of recent books published by Indian writers in India and abroad. Of the several qualities a book needs to have, is its capacity to capture the imagination of the reader. In other words, the most pertinent question is whether a book is 'readable.' The fiction of R.K. Narayan, Mulk

Raj Anand and Anita Desai has caught the attention of the audience for one or the other reason. Maybe an easy entry into the comic world, a deep concern with social problems, or face to face with the dilemmas of the woman's world. At the turn of the century, however, a new trend seems to be emerging. Marketing strategies are now as important as the contents of a book or its author. Modern technology, especially the media and the Internet, has played a significant role in promoting new books. This has been quite advantageous to the third-world writers, for their books reach the world over in no time. It is no longer uncommon to see a book on the day of its release selling at different places in different countries. Books are now being treated as revenue-generating products that need, apart from other ingredients, an author who has promotion potential and a publisher with wide marketing network. This development has helped an Indian writer in English much more than a regional Indian writer. Works of new writers like Salman Rushdie, Vikram Seth, Vikram Chandra, Gita Mehta, Rohinton Mistry and Arundhati Roy have been published by international book companies. Quality production, effective cost structure and easy mobility have given a boost to the sales: books are treated as products of a corpus culture, to be bought and sold with frenzied efforts. For example, *The Idea of India*, a diasporic book by India-born Oxford Professor Sunil Khilnani, has been listed by *The Guardian* among the best ten world books published in 1998.

Recently Sudhir Kakar, eminent psychiatrist and sexologist, has published his debut novel, *The Ascetic of Desire*. The time is the fourth century AD, the golden age of Indian history. The locale: an ashram in the woods a little outside Varanasi. Every morning Vatsyayana, author of the *Kamasutra*, recounts stories from his childhood and youth to a young pupil who plans to write the great sage's biography. Little is known of Vatsyayana's life, so the young scholar pieces these tales together along with relevant slokas of erotic wisdom from the *Kamasutra*, which he has learnt by heart.

The story that unfolds is fascinating. Vatsyayana's mother Avantika and her sister Chandrika are famous courtesans in a brothel at Kausambi. From them and their various lovers, Vatsyayana gains his first indelible impressions of sexual artifice. Later, Vatsyayana finds himself in an imbroglio of sexual passion and jealously involving his wife Malavika, the queen's sister, and her lover, a poet in King Udayana's court. Surprisingly, however, it turns out that Vatsyayana, the author of the world's best-known treatise on erotic techniques, is a sexual novice himself.

Increasingly, the pupil, who is embarking hesitantly on sexual exploits himself, finds to his consternation that his own life has begun to reflect and parallel the ascetic's narrative in many ways. Eventually, as the novel reaches its denouement, the two stories converge and collide, with disastrous results. Teacher and pupil part ways, and the biography remains unwritten, except for what is captured in the pupil's journal, which is *The Ascetic of Desire*.

With meticulous attention to historical detail, Sudhir Kakar's superb novel brings to life the reign of Samudragupta with all its pomp and grandeur. With characteristic insight, Kakar plumbs the psychological depths of a plethora of characters who are at various stages of discovering their sexual identities. What emerges through incidence and superimposition is a powerful narrative of lust and sensuality imbued with an old-world charm and a surprising sense of irony. A fitting fictional counterpart to the *Kamasutra, The Ascetic of Desire* is a major literary event of the year.

VII

Many of the regional writers too have been quite visible through translations. The translation phenomenon has become prominent, thanks to the efforts made by the Sahitya Akademi, Katha and other organizations. It has brought into cosmopolitan reckoning some of the brilliant writers in the regional languages. Indeed one of the most popular novels of recent times is U.R. Anantha Murthy's *Sanskara*, written originally in Kannada. The English translation by eminent poet A.K. Ramanujan may be construed as contribution both to traditional Indian literature as also to Indian English literature. The novel won the author many prestigious awards including the Sahitya Akademi and the Jnanpith Awards.

Several of the regional writers have captured the imagination of the English-speaking world. Translations of the plays by Girish Karnad, Vijay Tendulkar, Badal Sircar and Mohan Rakesh, novels by Premchand, R.N. Tagore, Sarat Chandra, Mahasweta Devi, Qurratulain Hyder, short stories by Sadat Hasan Manto and Krishan Chander have become immensely popular. Some years ago, Pakistani Urdu writer Intezar Husain was given the first Rupa Award of Rs. 50,000. The English translation of his short stories entitled *Leaves* became a favourite of the literary world.

VIII

The contemporary Indian poetry finds its source both from self and society. Poets like Nissim Ezekiel, Jayanta Mahapatra, Kamala Das, Keki Daruwalla have received international recognition. Recently Eunice de Souza has published a valuable book *Nine Indian Women Poets* (OUP). It introduces us to major contemporary women poets. The nine poets featured in this book represent two generations of Indian women poets of the post-1947 period.

Following Kamala Das almost every poet attempts to explore the self against a background of personal relationships. In Kamala Das's 'An Introduction,' the distinctiveness of possessing a language and the transmuting character of speech is submerged, perhaps even obliterated, by the experience of love.

Charmayne D'Souza writes about 'vivid inner experience rather than of localized spaces.' Her poems are imaginative, her themes varied and she gives the impression besides, and this again is rare, of greatly enjoying her writing. Her first collection *A Spelling Guide to Woman* was published in 1991 and one looks forward to reading more of this urbane and talented poet.

Another poet whose talent shines through clearly is Sujata Bhatt. Bhatt's is a highly personal poetry; she has a fine sense of the rhythms of language and is one of those poets who can fashion a poem out of almost anything.

IX

An appraisal of Indian drama shows that while drama in various Indian languages has shown a marked development, it has not done so in Indian English. In this literature, drama is a plant of poor growth. The first and the foremost reason is the want of a living theatre. It is a well-known fact that the real success of a play can be tested only on stage. A playwright needs a living theatre to put his work on acid test, evaluate its total effect on the audience and thereby get a chance to improve upon his performance. This handicap has not allowed him to pursue playwriting in a systematic and comprehensive way.

Very recently Indian English drama has shot into prominence. Younger writers like Mahesh Dattani and Manjula Padmanabhan have infused new life into this branch of writing. The thiry-eight-year-old Bangalore-based Dattani has published forceful plays like *Where There is a Will*, *Final Solutions* and *Tara*. Padmanabhan's Onassis award-winning *Harvest* has achieved worldwide acclaim. Incidentally, both Dattani and Padmanabhan do not write on the traditional subjects. Dattani writes about mean, ugly, unhappy things of life; Padmanabhan projects a dehumanized, terrifying world in which mothers sell their sons for "the price of rice." Her play *Harvest* is about an impoverished family living in a single room in a chawl of Bombay. Population explosion has rendered the city dwellers into helpless, poor, dehumanized lot struggling for their survival. In this scenario, driven by hunger and unemployment, twenty-year-old Om Prakash decides to become an organ donor and mortgages his body to a white First-World buyer. Padmanabhan projects in her play a more serious, grim and unpalatable world than Dattani. But her play is rather intellectual and not suited for stage, unlike the plays of Dattani which have been quite successful on the stage and have captured the imagination of the middle-class audience.

English plays are occasionally staged, especially in big cities like Bombay, Delhi and Calcutta. Visits of foreign troupes are arranged from time to time by the British Council and the American Center. In Delhi, Yatrik group has actively staged several plays. Barry John, the renowned director, has made a significant contribution to the Delhi theatre. It is a matter of great satisfaction that some of the Indian English plays like Gurcharan Das's *Mira*, Pratap Sharma's *A Touch of Brightness* and Asif Currimbhoy's *The Dumb Dancer* have been staged in the West.

It is mainly then Indian drama in Indian languages and the drama in English translation which has registered a remarkable growth in the recent decades. During the last few years, several plays originally written in the regional languages have been translated into English. Today, a sizeable number of such plays exist, and it is possible for the scholars to assess and evaluate Indian drama in its totality. Many academics have felt the need for English translations of literature in the Indian languages. English translations of classics in the Indian languages should form an important component of Indian English literature and if these are taught to our students, it will engage their attention fully and meaningfully. The translations have forged a link between the east and west, north and south, and contributed to the growing richness of contemporary creative consciousness. Thus regional drama in India is slowly paving way for a "national theatre" into which all streams of theatrical art seem to converge. The major language theatres active during the Sixties, Seventies and Eighties that rejuvenated and consolidated are those of Hindi, Marathi, Bengali and Kannada. A study of Vijay Tendulkar, Badal Sircar and Girish Karnad clearly shows that they are the symbols of the new resurgence in their own areas and have made bold innovations, fruitful experiments and given new directions which go in the history of Indian drama as a significant mark of achievement.

Novel Form in Ocean of Stories

MULK RAJ ANAND

Our forefathers were, for centuries, tellers of tales. So the earliest surviving fictions are stories of human foibles, proverbs with morals to teach folk way of good against evil. Tales were told and retold, but not written down. Creative imagination of bards, after Aryan penetration, elaborated two recitals in the Vedic and post-Vedic eras, the *Ramayana* and the *Mahabharata*. The themes of these epics are power struggles, In the *Ramayana*, the fabulous story of upperlands monarch, Rama in exile fights against Rakshasa Raja who abducts his Rani Sita. The *Mahabharata* has as its central theme the struggle against powerful Duryodhana for inheritance of share of kingdom, denied to younger Pandu cousins by the elder. There are several fictions assimilated in the *Mahabharata* like the love tale of Nala and Damyanti, of Savitri rescuing her spouse Satyavan from Yama. In fact it has been said, that what is not in the *Mahabharata* is insignificant.

In the later centuries, tales from the *Mahabharata* were adapted as plays, like *Shakuntala* by bard Kalidasa of fourth century A.D. In fact commentators of early medieval history laid down a dictum that all new fictions must be written about characters in the *Mahabharata*.

Apart from epics, which were recited in feudal courts, among the folk remained current fables and tales of words and deeds of Buddha. These short stories told in villages reached at a moral at the end of each tale. They remained popular lessons for preaching good against evil down the ages.

Brihut Katha stories were told by townfolk, also moral lessons to listeners to do good to others and speak truthfully. *Katha Sarit Sagar* or *Ocean of Stories*, tales told by counsellor Soma Deva to a dejected Rani, were current for centuries. Also there continued to be told Puranic myths by priests in temple gatherings, which showed struggle of Gods and Goddesses against Rakshasas, to infuse power for good of Gods against evil of power-mad Demons.

In the classical renaissance of the fourth/fifth centuries A.D., in royal courts, dramas came to be written on themes taken from epics, like *Shakuntala* by Kalidasa, which is drama of torment by cruel hero of innocent heroine when God Indra intervenes to restore love. But the denouement is still by God who helps the tormented.

Some plays like *Mrchakatika* by Sudraka, break away from divine sanctions and resolve conflict, through human struggle of righteous hero against men of evil intent. *Mudrarakshasa* dramatized the intrigues of crafty king-maker Chanakya.

In the eighth century appeared a novel entitled *Das Kumara* (*Ten Princes*) which is curiously an historical novel, the only one in the form of story telling tale without teaching moral at the end. At the core of fictions of early and medieval centuries, moral lessons remained dominant.

In the 19th century, there came into India, some novels from Imperial Britain, called escape literature, with which the British officials amused themselves in exile.

Bankim Chandra Chatterji was a graduate of the then-newly established Calcutta University. He read a novel entitled *Woman in White* by Wilky Collins. It is possible that he felt he could tell a love tale about Indian characters as in the English novel. So he wrote in English language his first novel *Rajmohan's Wife*, about ill-treatment of his spouse by an avaricious husband. As Bankim Chandra had experience of court cases about ownership of land in his capacity as Assistant Commissioner, he wrote a novel entitled *Krishan Kanta's Will* which reveals tussle about property in land in India where, in the old systems, no one owned land, but had rights to plough land. Bankim Chandra also wrote the first political novel in India about Sanyasi revolt against British exploitation, entitled *Anandmath*. Later, he wrote a historical novel about the love of Raja Man Singh's son for Durgesh Nandini, in the manner of Walter Scott, whose novels were coming into India at that time and were read voraciously by the isolated colonials.

Bankim Chandra remains the pioneer novelist of India, who accepted the form of eighteenth and nineteenth century British writers the novel of three dimensions, in which the novelist tells the story of say Moll Flanders, and, at the end, asks Dear Reader, not to do what the heroine did.

Our first Indian novelist did not know that, already in the nineteenth century, Charles Dickens, W.M. Thackeray and Thomas Hardy in England, had dropped the moral lesson of the eighteenth century novels and implied in the story itself human feelings against unethical behaviour.

Rabindranath Tagore, who took up the torch of Bankim Chandra, lit atmosphere of his novels and showed, through conflicting emotions of his characters, implicit in psychology what was for moral lesson in the novels of Fielding, Smollett, and Richardson. Tess had probably moved Thomas Hardy, who did not teach good ethics in his novel but told story of rape by the landlord's son of an innocent girl. Sensitive and penetrating poet Tagore made technical advance in novel form, by narrating feelings of his three characters Bimla, her liberal husband and Sandip, who fascinates the heroine with his eloquence, in the stream-of-consciousness of his characters. In this Tagore advanced novel form even before James Joyce and Virginia Woolf brought feelings of characters into play, without the author coming in as a moralist. In *Nauka Dubi (Wreck), Gora, Dui Bon* and other novels, Tagore took the technique of novel beyond three dimensions—into inner monologues, with no more lesson, except sensitive understanding.

After Tagore, as younger contemporary, Sarat Chandra went back to Bankim's manner of story telling in *Srikant*. In his short stories, he brought character from lower middle sections, widows, old men, bahus, with their woes in milieus where old conventions still lingered in a world unaffected by social reforms urged by Raja Ram Mohun Roy and the Brahmo Samaj.

The three Bannerjis who followed Sarat Chandra, took as theme new areas of life. Tara Shankar Bannerji recreated tribal characters. Bhibuti Bannerji brought into light villagers in his *Pather Pancholi* trilogy. Maneck Bannerji went into the lives of fisher folk.

Thematically, then, the novel form has gone deeper into obscure areas of the country beyond cities. Prem Chand ventured into the villages of upper India and miseries and deprivations of a peasant family in *Godan*. He was affected by the novels of Leo Tolstoy and the teachings of Gandhi. In his various novels and short stories Prem Chand made excursions into village lives, lower/middle sections and intricate bazaars of small towns, rendering up several characters who had hitherto not come into awareness of the epic novelist. Ratan Nath Sarshar in his *Fasana-i-Azad* which dealt with big upper feudal Zamindars. Prem Chand also noticed the plight of outcastes in his short stories and other rejects of caste society.

Shiv Ram Karanth chose to delineate the discarded in his novel about an outcaste in Kannada language. In several other fictions he revealed other rejected people under upper caste dominance.

Like his contemporaries Andre Malraux and Iqnezes Silon, Mulk Raj Anand reached lower depths for calm through his existentialist agony and later to self searches in novels of which the love is empathy from talismen of Gandhi to notice human condition in distress with his novel *Untouchable* which reached the unloved.

Successor of Shiv Ram Karanth, Anantha Murthy goes into the interior of Kannada folk, revealing decay and discrimination.

In Tamil Nadu there was, after poet patriot Bharati, writer of feelings, Venkataramani, who showed Murugan the peasant, toiling without reward and showed Gandhian concerns.

Among other writers in Karnataka, R.K. Narayan and Raja Rao emerged with new characters from small town life and villages affected by the waves of Gandhian awakening. R.K. Narayan, a detached observer, in his tales of Malgudi village, recreates obscure lives, of little people coming up for air, in frolic and fun. His novel *The Financial Expert* notices graft emergent among new merchants. In *Dark Room*, he notices the discontent of the wife, who sulks from the husband's unconcern but ultimately returns to traditional *Pati Seva* convention.

Raja Rao recreated in *Kanthapura* consciousness of folk, by legend of Gandhi, parallel to the lyrical creations of Francis Maureac and Jean Giono, turning inwards in his later novel *The Serpent and the Rope*.

In his second novel *Coolie*, written in reaction to the poet T.S. Eliot's praise of Kipling's novel *Kim*, Anand was to reveal a real orphan, crushed before he could grow into youth in a land where few white imperialists left millions in wretchedness beyond wretchedness, while they and their alien lived rich lives on high hills unmoved by the miseries below.

Anand's novels coincided with his initiative, along with the three Bannerjis, with the founding of the Progressive Writers' Association, of which the first President was Prem Chand. The movement was blessed by Jawaharlal Nehru, the author of *Glimpses of World History* and a masterly autobiography. Mahakavi Tagore presided over the second conference of All India Progressive Writers' Association. Manifestos of the Progressive Writers which seized upon human cause as the mainspring of new writings, was to find acceptances in various languages.

Sajjad Zaheer from among founders of Progressive Writers' Association led the younger poets Majaz, Jafri Faiz into eloquent expression of struggle to be truly human and extended empathies. Fiction writers from Punjab, Krishan Chander, Rajinder Singh Bedi, Saadat Hasan Manto extended their imaginative expressionism into lower middle millions. Ismat Chugtai was to recreate in novels and stories agonies of women behind the purdah.

In Malayalam language poet Valathol from his own empathies for the wretched, encouraged Shiv Shankar Pillai, Pottaket and other young writers. Shiv Shankar Pillai's novel about fisher folk *Chemeen*, Pottaket's stories, Ayyapa Paniker's critical writings, were imbued by love of those who had been kept traditionally down the ladder and kicked away if they ever tried to climb.

After the second world war, when imperialism retreated, awareness of miseries came to our intelligentsia by the partition of Punjab into *Tin Ab* and *Do Ab* by the evacuating power. And vital men of talent were affected by the killings. Khushwant Singh in his novel *Train to Pakistan* rendered the horrors committed by folk incensed against each other. Bhisham Sahni was to reveal terrors of the partition in a town in Punjab. Chaman Nahal in *Azadi* created, from motivations of his characters' suspicions, doubts, impulses of self-gain and misconceptions, chaos in which murder and exile showed death of human feelings.

Protest writings from high talents of the post-partition generations are emergent in our various languages, some of which have been honoured by Sahitya Akademi.

Consequent upon awareness of human rights, assured by constitution of free India, have come from among outcaste writers, condemned by taboos of orthodox Hinduism, with passionate poems, as also autobiographies like *Balut* by Daya Pawar.

Similar impulses of freedom to be and become have inspired women writers, Kamala Markandaya in *Nectar in a Sieve* and Kamala Das in *My Story*. Anita Desai and Nayantara Sahgal reveal discontent of women of middle sections against male assumption of prerogatives of superiority, strains of marriage among middle sections and disabilities forced on wives. Uma Vasudev shows of feudal lord and master in his conventional marital relations with a wife. Mahaswata Devi shows with intense passion violence of male against females of barbaric intensity in the story *Draupadi*. Shashi Deshpande goes into areas of discontent inherent in traditional dominations of male from neo-feminist attitudes, which show our women's defiance of conventional impositions. Conventions are emergent in eras in which political equality inspires struggles against impositions of shunned by shunners, of superiors on inferiors, from eras of contempt and denial of human space, to breathe air of freedom.

This brief survey of coming in of novel form in ocean of stories, integral development of various fictions, inevitable to the transition from human relations under feudal impositions and imperial dominance in eras of protest which showed questionings of younger intelligentsia the continuance under traditionalist cruelties.

It is likely that the novel form adopted by Indian creative writers will bring into light characters from several sections of our people.

Anand at 93: A Review

ALASTAIR NIVEN

He visited D.H. Lawrence shortly before the latter died. He worked with Leonard and Virginia Woolf as an amanuensis at the Hogarth Press. He lunched many times with T.S. Eliot, knew W.B. Yeats and H.B. Shaw and wrote a book of reminiscences called *Conversations in Bloomsbury.* E.M. Forster wrote the preface to his first novel. In the war years he was colleague of George Orwell at the B.B.C. His books sold by the million in the Soviet Union. Jawaharlal Nehru sought his opinions on affairs of state and Indira Gandhi called him 'Uncle.' He continues in his extreme old age to publish prolifically. Michael Foot led the tributes at a ninetieth birthday celebration in London held in sudabsentia. In 1996 he visited Britain on his own, though he has not lived here for fifty years. He is Mulk Raj Anand, born in Peshawar on 12 December 1905, now dividing his time between Bombay, Delhi and a hill station called Khandala. Still one of the best known contemporary Indians in his own country, he is little remembered in the United Kingdom, where he lived for the best part of twenty years and where, in the late 1930s, he briefly cut a fashionable figure.

In this age of international attention being paid to Indian novelists in the English language such as Vikram Seth, Amitav Ghosh and Arundhati Roy, it is difficult to envisage a time when some incredulity was expressed at the prospect of an author from the sub-continent essaying a work of fiction—this despite the fact that the first Indian novel, Bankim Chandra Chatterjee's *Rajmohan's Wife*, was published as early as 1864. Anand approached nineteen publishers in Britain before Forster's advocacy opened a door at the Marxist-orientated house of Lawrence and Wishart. *Untouchable*, which is invariably published with Forster's introduction and which has acquired classic status by any definition which can be applied to work by a living writer, came out in 1935. This is the same year which saw the publication of R.K. Narayan's first book, *Swami and Friends,* and only three years before Raja Rao's *Kanthapura,* which launched the third of the great trio of Indian novelists who between them created the genre of Indian English fiction which today has become so modish.

Untouchable gives us twenty-four hours in the life of a latrine cleaner in Bombay. Naomi Mitchison, in an undated letter written to Anand just after its publication, surmised that 'a good many people just won't read it, because of the dirt and cruelty you have conveyed in it.' This was not the India of nobos and mysticism which was usually described in fiction. Anand had depicted a rather different landscape of grim poverty, urban callousness and rigid social hierarchy in which someone literally outside caste was virtually a pariah, the key moment of the book being an accidental collision between the sweeper boy Bakha and caste Hindu to whom he forgets to announce himself with the admonitory 'posh, posh,' to indicate the proximity of an untouchable. Mitchison noted how Anand had written 'without any romanticising.' Forster, before publication when the novel's fate was still in doubt, put his reaction more graphically, in a letter he wrote to Anand on 6 May 1934: "It recalled to me very vividly the occasion I have walked 'the wrong way' in an Indian city, and it is a way down which no novelist has yet taken us. . . . The objection against the MS from the practical point of view seems to me not in its length but its 'squalor': I put this word in inverted commas as indicating that it doesn't convey my personal opinion, but it may well represent the opinion of the public."

The reading public never took to Anand as they were to do to Narayan, or later to Anita Desai or to Vikram Seth, but among writers he was greatly admired in both Britain and India. V.S. Pritchett, for example, gave Anand's second novel *Coolie* a favourable review in *London Mercury* (Vol. 34, August 1936) and in a letter to Anand a few months later wrote, "I got more out of *The Coolie* (sic) than out of any other novel I have read for a very long time indeed. . . . *The Coolie* is the only 'political' novel I have read which profoundly satisfied me." These first books by Anand were translated into many languages. Quite early on, however, he was also often dismissed by critics as an agitator or didactician, particularly in India where his proletarian characters and his espousal of social reforms based on a mixture of Gandhian and Marxist principles were not in tune with academic literary values distilled from the Oxford of Maurice Bowra.

Anand reserved his more overt socialism for his novels. Sometimes the titles alone are an indication of this. *The Sword and the Sickle*, for example, which was published in 1942, as the third part of a trilogy focussing upon a young peasant called Lalu. There was *Two Leaves and a Bud* (1937), which drew from the critical comments in the Whitley Report—the Royal Commission on Labour—in its accounts of how workers were treated on the tea plantations, and *The Big Heart* (1945), an account of union formation among coppersmiths and full of oblique acknowledgements to Ernst Toller's *The Machine Wreckers*. Outstanding among these early novels is *Across the Black Waters* (1940), in some ways my personal favourite among all his writings because in it Anand utters the pity of war without flamboyance or sentimentality. The middle part of the Lalu trilogy, between *The Village* (1939) and *The Sword and the Sickle*, it depicts Indian sepoys in the trenches of the First World War, when they neither knew nor cared about the issues and personalities which the war was about. Although the story of Indian soldiers in the world wars has now begun to be told—in *Dusky Warriors* (1995), a play by Kulvinder Ghir and Nasser Memarzia, for example—no one has caught better than Anand the bewilderment and occasional deracinated comedy of the soldiers who were shipped to Flanders as human cannon fodder. Of all his novels it is the one which most merits rediscovery, because it would inform many kinds of postcolonial discourse from a perspective that has been little appreciated.

This novelist who is so often regarded as a slightly simplistic champion of peasant rights has in fact been extraordinarily wide-ranging in his subject matter. His finest novel may well be *Private Life of an Indian Prince* (1953), his last to be published in its first edition in Britain. The fate of the Indian aristocracy after independence might not have been thought an obvious subject for a novelist also identified with Indian liberationist aspirations. In *Private Life of an Indian Prince*, however, Anand created in Victor, the Maharaja Ashok Kumar, a pitiable, complex, valetudinarian character who is impaled both on the political circumstances of the Raj's demise and on the rack of his own impulsive passions. He loses everything and descends into a madness echoing Lear's. On the way to evoking Vicky's personal nadir, Anand treats the great political losses of the princes with far more compassion than anyone knowing his work only from the earlier novels could have anticipated. This, however overlooks his erudition, seldom displayed in his fiction but manifest in many books and essays published in the preceding twenty-three years: *Persian Painting* (1930), *The Hindu View of Art* (1933), *The Story of India* (1948), and *The Indian Theatre* (1950), to say nothing of his founding and editing of *Marg,* which for a long time was India's leading visual arts journal. In publications such as these, a deep knowledge of Indian history and aesthetics indicate a man far more sophisticated in his understanding of the inter-relationships of Indian society over many centuries than that sometimes portrayed by derogatory literary critics. This acknowledgement of the contributions of royalty to India's culture, as well as to her social inequities, distinguish Anand from routine social polemicists and in particular mark out *Private Life of an Indian Prince* as a serious reflection on India's transition from fiefdom to nation.

Although nothing subsequently written by Anand has received serious notice in the western press, he has in the last forty years produced several books which in any assessment of his work must be regarded as crucial. Indeed, in my own study, *The Yoke of Pity: the Fictional Writing of Mulk Raj Anand* (1978), I approached his authorial career through the sequence of novels currently given the working title *And So He Plays His Part.* This so far comprises four books, *Seven Summers* (1951), *Morning Face* (1968), *Confession of a Lover* (1976) and *The Bubble* (1984), as well as *Little Plays of Mahatma Gandhi* (1990), which show Anand experimenting at this late stage of his career more radically with form than ever before. In these works he creates a confessional character called Krishan Chander Azad whose life approximates to Anand's.

Real characters people the novels—the writers, fellow students, politicians, lovers and village folk who have been part of Anand's personal odyssey. Diatribes and conversations are re-constructed. Letters and diaries are interpolated. It may be that at Anand's advanced age his project, which is planned to be seven lengthy novels exploring the seven ages of man, will not be completed, but already it is a landmark in that twentieth-century genre, the bildungsroman.

Mulk Raj Anand's historic importance is already established and it is hard to believe that it will be ignored in the future. Along with Narayan and Rao, he virtually created the modern Indian novel in English and brought it to international as well as pan-Indian attention. In that extraordinarily long-living generation, which also includes the mandarin autobiographer, historian and essayist Nirad C. Chaudhuri, who was one hundred years old on 23 November 1997. Anand stands out as the most wide-ranging and prolific. Though not primarily a dramatist, Anand's best comparitor is perhaps George Bernard Shaw. He occupies in India something of that 'awkward cuss' reputation, which can be mocked but not dismissed. Like Shaw's, his work is unfashionable, yet literary histories, at least in India, give it prominence. Again like Shaw he is a compulsive correspondent who must write scores of animated letters a week all over the world.

In novels such as *Coolie* and *The Village*, Anand more effectively than perhaps any of the major Indian writers found a hybrid language to suggest in English the rhythms and nuances of a mother tongue, in his case Punjabi. Yet as *Private Life of an Indian Prince* demonstrates, he can be the master of aristocratic portraiture too. I regard him not as an unsung writer—he is far too famous in India to be that—but as one whom the literary pantheonists are in danger of placing in some neglected catacomb off a side aisle. He is in truth a figure of towering humanity whose work guides us through the multitudinous complexity of India this century with more verve than any other prose writer of his time.

Historical Text, Human Context: Khushwant Singh's *Train to Pakistan*

V.T. GIRDHARI

The novel is the history of human experiences.

Joseph Conrad

Khushwant Singh's picture of Indian society in *Train to Pakistan* is like the state of Eden before and after the Fall. Symbolic Eden is Mano Majra and the date of the Fall is summer of '47: "When the creation of the new state of Pakistan was formally announced,' it 'was not like other Indian summers. Even the weather had a different feel in India that year. It was hotter than usual, and drier and dustier . . . for weeks, the clouds cast only shadows. There was rain. People began to say that God was punishing them for their sins."[1]

The life in Mano Majra is punctuated by the morning and evening train to and from Lahore when it is time for the mullah at mosque to offer morning prayer facing Mecca towards west with his sonorous notes of "Allah-ho-Akbar" and the Sikh priest responding by his prayer while splashing water over himself from the well in Gurudwara compound. Evening views the same chore after which the life in Mano Majra is stilled. This was the paradoxical state of Mano Majra until the summer of '47. Even the sub-inspector confides to Hukumchand that no one in Mano Majra knew that the British had left India and the country was divided into Pakistan and Hindustan. There are the reports of riots and retaliations from various parts of the country and Hukumchand's subtle question 'how long will it be before it starts here,' strikes the keynote. Sub-inspector throws in the feeler that there were some

Muslim families in every Sikh village like Mano Majra. One has to read this novel in a very broad social perspective.

Train to Pakistan is not just a political novel but a social one—a politics-polluted society, played with by the bureaucrats for their personal and private ends, under the pretensions of executing the so-called policies of the so-called Government. After all what are Hukumchands and sub-inspectors?—mere helpless instruments for execution of law. Despite their apparent manipulations and manoeuvrings they are all human beings. Khushwant Singh appears to bless them all and forgive them all with his Christ-like compassion. Love is the only redeeming grace of human life, the only impulse to which one and all respond instinctively. Hukumchand's love for Haseena Begum not only creates moral compunctions in him but makes him change his ways only if to save the train in which Haseena is to leave for Pakistan. He releases Jugga Badmash and Iqbal whose arrest order he himself had signed and had also justified it to himself. The love of Jugga for Nooran is a saga of human sufferings and sacrifice elevated to epic grandeur. Jugga's struggle and ultimate death to save the train in which Nooran is supposed to be travelling to Pakistan is truly Greek in its catastrophic effect.

Khushwant Singh's transcendental views on love as an ultimate expression of life and its truth enable him not to harp upon Juggatsingh as a criminal or Hukumchand as a corrupt bureaucrat. He treats them simply as human beings. Sin is their share of life, hence the suffering. The process of introspection in the mind of Hukumchand, while with Haseena, young enough to be his daughter, shows him a better human being than all the immoralities and corruptions put together can show him as a brute. The stream of his thoughts at the sight of so many dead gives a right comprehension of his consciousness, his broader sense of human values. He suffers like Buddha at the sight of so much pain and suffering, decay and death: "It was everyone's destiny. . . . He had watched young and old brought on crude bamboo stretchers, lamented for, and then burned. Visits to the cremation ground left him with a sense of tranquillity. He had got over the immediate terror of death, but the idea of ultimate dissolution was always present in his mind. It made him kind, charitable and tolerant. It even made him cheerful in adversity." (76)

The departure of Muslims from Mano Majra is another scene symbolic of human solidarity and faith. Two communities had been there together for centuries with their lives in such a well-knit social and personal pattern that the thought of one community leaving brought tears to both. It is so gratifyingly pathetic to see Sikhs greeting Muslims with "Salaam" and Muslims wishing them back with 'Sat Sri Akal.' In spite of all the turmoil around, Sikhs assure Muslims: "As long as we are here nobody will dare touch you." Imam Baksh breaks down—what they had to do with Pakistan? They were born here, so were their ancestors. They had lived amongst Sikhs as brothers. All fell into each others' arms and cried. "This is life . . . this is the way of the world":

> Not forever does the bulbul sing
> In balmy shades of bowers,
> Not forever lasts the spring
> Nor ever blossom flowers.
> Not forever reigneth day,
> Sets the sun on days of bliss,
> Friendships not forever last,
> They know not life, who know not this. (112)

Most of the people in Mano Majra did not sleep that night. They kept moving from house to house—talking, crying, swearing love and friendship. This is Khushwant Singh's vision of life—comic in thought and tragic in feeling. All the situations and the characters therein embody this vision. Nature, with its whims and vagaries, does not appear just for its aesthetic value but represents the changing situations of human lives regulated by politics-dominated civilization. Rhythmic pattern of this change, in terms of time motion, is symbolized by the train. The train is the hopeful conveyor of the masses from both sides of territorial divisions to their respective heavens of hope. Their roots losing their grip over the native soil, men, women and children on the move in search of a new home, a new harbour, a new identity, is a pathetic process of disintegration of human lives segregated by the decisions not their own. Khushwant Singh observes:

> Early in September the time schedule in Mano Majra started going wrong. Trains became less punctual than ever before and many more started to run through at night. Some days it seemed as though the alarm clock had been set for the 'wrong hour.' On others, it was as if no one had remembered to wind it. Imam Baksh waited for Meet Singh to make the first start. Meet Singh waited for the mullah's call to prayer before getting up. People stayed in bed late without realizing that times had changed and the mail train might not run through at all. Children did not know when to be hungry, and clamoured for food all the time. In the evenings, everyone was indoors before sunset and in bed before the express came by—if it did come by. Good trains had stopped running altogether, so there was no lullaby to lull them to sleep. Instead, ghost trains went past at odd hours between midnight and dawn, disturbing the drams of Mano Majra. (67)

Nature too seems to respond to and sympathize with the plight of human beings:

> The sun behind the bridge, lighting the white clouds which had appeared in the sky with hues of russet, copper and orange. Then shades of gray blended with the glow as evening gave way to twilight and twilight sank into darkness. The station became a black wall. Wearily, the men and women went down to their courtyards, beckoning the others to do the same. They did not want to be alone in missing anything. . . . That evening, for the first time in the memory of Mano Majra, Imam Baksh's sonorous cry did not rise to the heavens to proclaim the glory of God. (73)

Hukumchand, lying lonely in his rest house, brooded over a glass of whisky, watching lizards and moth with their shining black eyes. 'Perhaps that was its destiny,' he thought 'it was everyone's destiny.' He realized that, 'that was life, and it was very depressing.'

There is a comic side too, to Khushwant Singh's view of life. His day-light sun-bright, broad humour, his extra-overtones and robust 'nar-admi' hopefulness and faith in innate goodness of man have its native roots in Punjabi ethos. Jugga is an incorrigible Don Quixote to suffer the physical indignities at the hands of police with a pinch of salt and acceptance but is a serious lover in the next moment ready to lay down his life, for love, without a second thought. He feels it an act of affrontry and stain on his personal honour when Malli, an outsider, commits murder in his village Mano Majra. The Punjabi's code was that truth, honour, financial integrity were 'all right,' but these were placed

> lower down the scale of values than being true to one's salt, to one's friends and fellow villagers. For friends you could lie in court or cheat, and no one would blame you. On the contrary, you became a nar admi—a he-man who had defied authority (magistrates and police) and religion (catch on the scripture) but proved true to friendship. It was the projection of rural society where everyone in the village was relation and loyalty to the village was the supreme test. (37)

Hukumchand accepted gifts and obliged friends when they were in trouble, but he was not corrupt. He even joined parties for dancing and singing—sometimes sex, but he was not immoral. That was the core of his philosophy of life, says Khushwant Singh.

Very typically Indian are the colloquial obscenities like 'sala' and 'susra,' the terms of love and intimacy amongst friends. Every topic of talk leads ultimately to sex, which everyone enjoys with a lot of "giggling and handslapping." Khushwant Singh's literal translations of obscenities related to sister and mother have been used so spontaneously that they seem to have lost their bitterness.

In Khushwant Singh's world of realities, life is not monopolized by either of the two forces—tragic and comic—life is a harmonious fusion of the two.

NOTE

1. Khushwant Singh, *Train to Pakistan* (Pearl Paperback Edition, Bombay: India Book House), p. 1.

Mythical Intention in Vikram Seth's *A Suitable Boy*

R. RADHIGA PRIYADHARSHINI

Every great work of art is a perfect unity of words and images. Just as a poet is brought up to speak and write one particular language, he is also brought up in one particular religion or culture. Divergent cultural heritage of India offers many such myths and archetypes for a sensitive writer like Vikram Seth.

In his *A Suitable Boy*,[1] Vikram Seth consciously utilizes the various myths and archetypes to give meaning to the social, political and cultural milieu of India. He concentrates on the original imaginative life of the myths and gives meaning to the *ethos* of the novel ironically. Beginning in realism, the irony steadily moves to myth and dim outlines of rituals reappear in ironic mode. This reappearance of myth in the ironic is obvious in *A Suitable Boy*, as it elaborates certain rituals of Hindus and Muslims.

The novel starts with the marriage of Savitha and ends with that of Lata. The garden of 'Prem Nivas' is the locale of Savitha's marriage with Pran. It is presented as the displaced version of the Edenic garden. The original good nature before the Fall is conveyed through the auspicious stars above. The garden with the Tree of Life (harsingar tree) and the holy fire accompanied by the holy mantras connecting the heaven and the earth give a sense of elevated feelings. But Lata considers it ironical to call the house 'Prem Nivas,' an abode of love, where only arranged marriages take place. The next moment Lata changes her attitude and thinks:

> Perhaps this little fire was indeed the Centre of the Universe.

> For here it burned, in the middle of the fragrant garden, itself in the heart of Pasand Bagh, the pleasantest locality of Brahmpur, which was the capital of the State of Purva Pradesh, which lay in the centre of the Gangetic plains, which was itself the heartland of India . . . and so on through the galaxies to the outer limits of perception and knowledge. (15)

The sudden change in Lata's attitude decides the direction of the future events in the novel. Her love for Kabir, a Muslim boy, which takes place in libraries, book shops and symposiums reaches its climax on their trip to Barsaat Mahal. Their love cannot exist on the land. They need a different element. We are reminded of the small boat which braves the rain and wind in *A Farewell to Arms* while reading about the boating expedition of Lata and Kabir. He tells Lata his experience in Gulmarg.

> What I meant was that you're in a completely different element. All your movements are different—and, as a result, all your thoughts. When I went tobogganing in Gulmarg once, I remember thinking that I didn't really exist. All that existed was the clean, pure air, the high snows, this rush of swift movement. The flat, drab plains bring you back to yourself. Except, perhaps, well, like now on the river. (166)

The boatman comments that the land-bound people are insane. The boat contains the precious life principle, love, only for a while. It does not carry it through the dissolution to time like Noah's ark. It comes back to land. The lovers are seen by somebody and the news reaches Mrs. Rupa Mehra's ears. She takes Lata to different places in search of a suitable boy. This trip makes a total change in Lata's view of life and life in India. Lata accepts Haresh, her mother's choice, as a suitable boy and tells Malathi: "Haresh's feet touch the ground, and he was dust and sweat and a shadow. The other two [Amit, the poet and Kabir, her lover] are a bit too God-like and ethereal to be any good for me." (129) After Savitha's marriage, the novelist takes the reader far and wide over India's social and political scenario and contrives to end the trip with Lata's marriage to Haresh.

While the marriage ceremony takes place in Lata's maternal grandpa's garden, Kabir takes a long walk on the banks of Ganga. On that day Kabir should have visited his insane mother. But he seeks the company of water, the Great Mother, where the deep pull of unconscious dissolves the self in something greater than the self. The great linga the King of Marh tries to excavate from the earth also rolls down on the bank of Ganga and is finally submerged in the river. In mythology, the castrated phallus or linga of Shiva goes deep under the earth causing chaos and disorder over the cosmos. The devas and rishis descend down to keep it on a vase, a female symbol. Here the linga is not, according to the plan of Raja, installed on the western side of the mosque. The linga's disappearance into the water connotes the absence of the concord in the Man and Wife relationship. Right from Lata's maternal grandpa's mismatched second marriage to Rasheed's marrying his deceased brother's wife, there are unequal and unhappy marriages. The world of *A Suitable Boy* is male-dominated. But through the submerged linga, the writer gives an ambivalent perception of the patriarchal society. The linga or the active, dominating masculine Will of Life seems to find its rest in Ganga, the maternal matrix of Life. It is contrary to the traditional picture of Shiva holding Ganga in his matted hair.

The matriarchal Indian society with its "Great Mother" at the centre is symbolized through Mrs. Mahesh Kapoor. Apparently the world of *A Suitable Boy* is men-oriented. But the ultimate truth is that it is anchored to the world of women. Mrs. Mahesh Kapoor is pictured at the beginning of the novel as a shy, insignificant lady, but her death brings out very powerfully what she had been to the home and the world.

> fat, ligament, muscle, blood, hair, affection, pity, despair, anxiety, illness: all were no more. She had dispersed. She was the garden at Prem Nivas . . . she was Veena's love for music, Pran's asthma, Maan's generosity, the survival of some refugees four years ago, the neem leaves that would preserve quilts stored in the great zinc trunks of Prem Nivas, the moulting feather of some pond-heron, a small unrung brass bell, the memory of decency in an indecent time. (1120)

At her death-ritual, Mahesh Kapoor is amazed to see the crowd which came to pay homage to her, "whom he had always thought of as being silly, superstitious and limited woman." (1221) The novel is pervaded with the feminine will of Mrs. Rupa Mehra, who is a mother not only to her children but also to all who come in contact with her. The Nawab of Baitar who in his audacity of youth violated Saeeda Bai's youth turned to religion and scholarly pursuits due to the quiet influence of his wife who was always behind the purdah.

In contrast to the preserving "Great Mother" exemplified in characters like Mrs. Mahesh Kapoor and Mrs. Rupa Mehra, is created Saeeda Bai, a courtesan gazal singer. Maan, the younger son of Mahesh Kapoor, becomes a slave to Saeeda Bai when she gives a music performance at Prem Nivas on Holi. Her rich clothes and precious stones bring to mind the idea of "the Great Whore" presented by Northrop Frye: "The Great Whore's rich clothes and precious stones recall the gilded serpent; she represents all human tyranny, for her name is Babylon . . . and her whoredom represents the possessive love of the jealous selfhood. She is in short, the ultimate fallen form of nature or the "female will."[2] The enticing female will is the centre of attraction on the spring festival, Holi. "She looked stunning . . . she moved the pallu of her silk further forward over her head: it tended to slip down, and one of her most charming gestures—to be repeated throughout the evening—was to adjust her sari to ensure that her head was not left uncovered." (79)

The veil which half conceals and half reveals her beauty is what Blake calls "Vala" or Veil between himself and reality. She is the displaced Mayadevi or the goddess of illusion in Hindu mythology or the *femme fatale* of romantic poets whose kiss is death and whose unanswerable riddle of life is reflected in the mysterious female smiles of Sphinx and Mona Lisa. Maan is the Man susceptible to the temptation of this force and he becomes fallen.

Firoz (Nawab's son) falls in love with Tasneem, the supposed sister of Saeeda Bai, who was actually born to her by the Nawab. Maan follows Firoz to Saeeda Bai's house and asks whether he was in love with Tasneem, her sister. On hearing this, Saeeda laughs frantically, repeating, "it is not my *sister* he is in love with—it is not *my* sister he is in love with." Maan could not understand the implied meaning and comes to the hasty conclusion that she has betrayed him with his friend and starts attacking her. Firoz interferes and receives the wound. With the pain of the wound and the shock of the news that Tasneem was his sister, he staggers out of Saeeda Bai's house leaving a trail of blood behind him. The blood-trail resembles *The Old Testament* story of the harlot Rahab who ties a scarlet thread to her window to denote her house, when Joshua comes in quest of the Promised Land. But in the ironic world of *A Suitable Boy* the blood-trail betrays the visit of Nawab's son to the whore. In the mythical world, Joshua was the prototype of Jesus. Here, Firoz is the displaced Jesus who bleeds for the sins of his parent.

The ironic scene goes in coincidence with Saeeda Bai's comparison of Firoz with Hussain and Tasneem with Zainab, the mythical hero's sister. Firoz gets another wound (the first wound) when the tazia procession (which laments the death of Hussain) cuts across Bharat Milaap procession (which celebrates the meeting of Ram and Bharat) and creates a communal riot between Hindus and Muslims. The cutting of the two processions by each other brings to one's mind the cross imagery and Firoz bleeds like Jesus or Hussain for the sins of his fellow-men.

On the way to the Promised Land or the Land of Self-Realization one has to face the Great Whore whose veil has to be torn asunder. For Maan and Firoz, the veil of selfhood falls down at a crucial hour of revelation at the house of Saeeda Bai. The veil of mystery is torn asunder and they behold life as it is. In the mythical world of *The Old Testament*, Rahab married Joshua and their children were to be the prophets. But in the ironic world of *A Suitable Boy*, Saeeda Bai sings a song of herself, the song of the player through whom the eternal game of hide and seek is endlessly played in time. She sings:

> The meeting has dispersed; the moths
> Bid farewell to the candle-light.
> Departure's hour is on the sky.
> Only a few stars make the night.

What has remained will not remain:
They too will quickly disappear,
This is the world's way, although we,
Lost to the world, lie sleeping here. (1315)

This song is followed by another song, and we know not who sings this. Maybe it is the song of eternity. The waters of Ganga are flowing from somewhere to nowhere.

No satan, no God, no Iblis, no Gabriel.
Endless, endless, endless, the waters of Ganga.
The stars above, below.

. . . and some were seized by the Cry, and some
We made the earth to swallow, and some
We drowned; God would never wrong them, but
they wronged themselves. (1315)

This anonymous song sung in the presence of Ganga and Rasheed does not blame fate, God or anything but places Man at the helm of the affair and here lies the success of the artist.

Vikram Seth, like Kafka and Joyce, makes his mythical intention clear. But for the ironic myth, the story would appear to be meaningless. Northrop Frye comments: "However, ironic myth is frequent elsewhere, and many features of ironic literature are unintelligible without it. Henry James learned his trade mainly from the realists and naturalists of the nineteenth century, but if we were to judge, for example, the story called *The Altar of the Dead* purely by low mimetic standards, we should have to call it a tissue of improbable coincidence, inadequate motivation, and inconclusive resolution."[3] The mythical intention in *A Suitable Boy* not only reveals the irony but also makes the structure simple and logical.

NOTES

1. Vikram Seth, *A Suitable Boy* (New Delhi: Penguin India, 1993).
2. Northrop Frye, *Fearful Symmetry: A Study of William Blake* (New Jersey: Princeton UP, 1947), pp. 139-49.
3. Northrop Frye, *Anatomy of Criticism: Four Essays* (New Jersey: Princeton UP, 1971), pp. 42-43.

Disappearances and Discovery: A Study of Amitav Ghosh's *The Calcutta Chromosome*

INDIRA BHATT

'Malaria strikes back' screams the head-lines in newspapers, periodicals, scientific journals. Teams of research-journalists re-record the details from the past—the historical facts about malaria and the scientist Sir Ronald Ross who was awarded the Nobel Prize for his findings on malarial fever. This sets off the creative artist into the jungle of science-laboratories, scientific vocabulary, the methods of investigation and the scientists. Amitav Ghosh in his novel *The Calcutta Chromosome*[1] takes up this issue of the malarial fever colouring it with mysticism and mystery, supernatural and superstition, calling it the theory of science and counter-science:

> "Let me put it like this," Murugan said. "You know all about matter and anti-matter, right? And rooms and anterooms and Christ and anti-Christ and so on? . . . Now let's say there was something like science and counter-science? Thinking of it in the abstract, wouldn't you say that the first principle of a functioning counter-science would have to be secrecy? The way I see it, wouldn't just have to be secretive about *what* it did (it couldn't hope to beat the scientists at the game anyway); it would have to be secretive *in* what it did. It would also have to use secrecy as a technique of procedure. It would in principle have to refuse all direct communication, straight off the bat, because to communicate, to put ideas into language would be to establish a claim to *know*—which is the first thing that a counter-science would dispute." (88)

Murugan further explains:

> Not making sense is what it's about, conventional sense that is. Maybe this other team started with the ideas that knowledge is self-contradictory, maybe they believed that to know something is to change it, therefore in knowing something, you've already changed what you think you know so you don't really know it at all: You only know its history. Maybe they thought that knowledge couldn't begin without acknowledging the impossibility of knowledge." (88)

Thus he arrives at the working hypotheses: "If it's true that to know something is to change it, then it follows that one way of changing something—of effecting a mutation, let's say—is to attempt to know it or aspect of it." (88) With this Amitav Ghosh emphasizes secrecy, mystery and self-contradictory knowledge and confronts what he calls conventional science with the ingenious knowledge and method of the uneducated Indians. This paper attempts to examine how this theory of science and counter-science is presented and with what purpose.

It is Murugan the Indian scientist working in New York's Life-Watch, an expert on Ronald Ross and malarial fever who narrates the story to Antar the Egyptian technologist working alone from his flat in New York with his computer AVA as per the instructions of his employer, the International Water Council. Murugan and his story are screened, shown to Antar who has simply to push some buttons and AVA goes hunting all the details about Murugan, his movements, his ideas, his beliefs, his suppositions and inferences. This happens cinemategraphically, Antar watching sort of a film as we do, so often on TV screen. Only this is the twenty-first century and the method and manner of the show is quite different. The novel opens sometime in early 21st century in Antar's flat in New York with the appearance of an ID card on AVA's screen which tripped her system and she wouldn't stop till she found out all about the subject: Like why? What? When? Where? How? She has some sort of a simulated urge for self-improvement. Ghosh describes this system of the future minutely: "Anything she didn't recognize she'd take apart on-screen, producing microscopic structural analyses, spinning the images around and around, tumbling them over, resting them on their side, producing ever greater refinements of details." (3-4) and further he clarifies that "she had been programmed to hunt out *real-time* information, and that was what she was determined to get. Once she'd wrung the last, meaningless detail out of him, she'd give the object on her screen, final spin, with a bizarrely human smugness, before propelling it into the horizonless limbo of her memory." (4)

This sets the tone of the novel and provides explanations of all sorts of details made known to Antar (and to the reader) surmised and inferred by Murugan, about the events that happened in 1995 in Calcutta as also some hundred years ago in Calcutta and Hyderabad. Ghosh has used this device of computer-system of the future, like H.G. Wells' Time-machine, to move in time-past, recent past and present for Antar. For the reader it is past—the last decade of the 19th century, the present days of August 1995 and the Future sometime in early part of the 21st century. He has manipulated the time-span, as Malcolm Bradbury explains: "an exploitation of relation between antecedent and present, between the time-span, of what is told and the time it takes to tell, between narrated time and narrational time, between matter attended to scenically and in detail and matter scanted or sketched."[2] It takes only a few hours for Antar to watch Murugan's experiences of two days in Calcutta and what Murugan explains of experiments of Ronald Ross and others, a few years of the 19th century. It is at three levels of time that the story is revealed to the reader, unfolded as it is through AVA. It also involves a high degree of 'fictional faking' and the novelist tries to create a sense of mystery and a special insight into the oriental sense of spiritualism, belief in birth and rebirth, transposition and transcendence which is no more than a numinously dramatic satisfaction, "a building up of the so called myth its own splendid sake."[3]

Against the background of the historical facts of Ronald Ross's discovery about malarial fever, the novelist presents the supernatural power of Mangala, an assistant to D.D. Cunningham. She is portrayed as a goddess-like figure who has found a so-called cure for siphilis but has also acquired knowledge of transcending life beyond life. The two parallel events are described: Mangala sometime in 1893 performs certain rituals (recorded in a letter by Farley): "What he [Farley] saw was this: the woman Mangala was seated at the far end of the room, on a low divan, but alone and in an attitude of command, as though enthroned. By her side at the far end of the room were several bamboo cages, each containing a pigeon . . . they were all slumped on the floors of their cages, shivering, evidently near death . . . on the floor by the divan, clustered around the woman's feet, were some half-dozen people in various attitudes of supplication, some touching her feet, others lying prostrate. Two or three others were huddled against the wall, wrapped in blankets . . . they were syphilitics, in final stages of the terrible disease." (125-26) Farley the western scientist understands this clearly and wants to warn them not to waste their hopes on "Whatever" quackery it was that the woman offered, to expose the falsehoods that she and her minions had concocted to deceive those simple people. (126) But his curiosity makes him stay where he was, unobserved by Mangala and sit through Mangala's performance of rituals. Finally he returns to his own experiment and demands to see the slides 'the transformations that Laveran described.' Only after that he is given the slides smeared with the dying pigeon's blood: "it was then that he saw Laveran's rods appear, hundreds of them, tiny cylindrical things, with their pointed penetrating heads piercing the blood miasma." (128) This was to be the future invention of his team-mates. His knowledge proves his doom. He is promised by Mangala through the young boy assistant to reveal everything "if I would but accompany him to his birth place, fortunately the place of which he spoke is not far from the location of my clinic. We are to leave to-morrow." (129) But Elijah Farley never reaches Barich; he disappeared during the journey, never to be seen again. "The police discovered that he had indeed boarded the train at Sealdah, as scheduled but had disembarked before his destination—a remote rarely used station called Renupur, in severe monsoon weather. A guard was said to have reported later that a young man had been seen carrying his luggage." (129) He is denied knowledge. His glimpse into Mangala's knowledge is the cause for his disappearance—death. Even the letter he wrote from which Murugan constructs the story of Farley's and Mangala's encounter, disappears and there is no scientific proof of Farley's knowledge and experiment as also about the existence of the letter. Cleverly the novelist constructs mystery both about Farley's knowledge and his disappearance.

A similar event takes place in 1995. It is Sonali who goes looking for Roman Haldar to the old house at Robinson street which Romen had shown her. Her experience and observation of the rituals are recorded:

> She caught a glimpse of tops of dozens of heads, some male, some female, young and old, packed in close together. Their faces were obscured by the smoke and flickering firelight. . . . Then there was a stir in the crowd and Sonali forced herself to look down again. A figure had come out of the shadows: it was a woman and she was dressed very plainly—in a crispy-starched saree, with a white scarf tied around her hair. Her figure was short and matronly and Sonali took her to be in late middle age . . . she had a cloth bag slung over one shoulder, an ordinary cotton jhola, in her left hand she was carrying a bamboo bird-cage. She seated herself by the fire and placed the bag and the bird-cage beside her. She took out two scalpels and a pair of glass plates. Then she reached out, placed her hands on whatever it was lying before the fire and smiled. Raising her voice, the woman said to the crowd, in archaic rustic Bengali: 'The time is here, pray that all goes well for our Laakhan once again' . . . there was a flash of bright metal and a necklace of blood flew up and fell sizzling on the fire. (139-40)

The body on which the rituals are performed is that of Romen Haldar and the woman is Mrs. Aratounian who does not speak, to Sonali's knowledge, Bengali. Romen Haldar who was to meet Sonali that evening, suddenly and inexplicably disappears. The novelist does not explain his death or what he keeps on calling, disappearance. These two events separated by hundred years adds to the mystification of the plot in the novel. In the case of Farley, it is his knowledge which is to be kept secret that brings about his disappearance—death. In Haldar's case, nothing is mentioned, except that in the Calcutta of 1995 such mysterious rituals are performed in the name of some special knowledge of transcendence. Then there is the mention of a station-master who gets killed at Renupur (where Farley had been killed in 1894) on a moonless Amavasya night possibly in the year 1900, at the hands of a boy called Laakhan. In 1933 or so Phulboni miraculously saves himself from getting killed by the train at Renupur. Way back in 1895 in Secunderabad Grigson had also with great difficulty saved himself from getting killed just like Phulboni in 1933. Both of them were followed by the railway station lantern and could not see who was trying to kill them, though Lutchman and Laakhan are mentioned. Phulboni in his stories mentions Laakhan and the ghost-trains that he himself had seen, the ghost-station-master that he had come across. The characters Lutchman, Laakhan, Lucky of the 19th, the 20th and the 21st centuries appear and disappear. Are we to suppose, according to the novelist's theory voiced through the character of Murugan, that they are improvements on their earlier life? There are no such indications in the novel. In fact these characters are not even fully presented three dimensional characters. There is also a hint that the boy who appears at Urmila's doorstep with fish wrapped in papers from which Murugan connects up the story is the same one Laakhan. So it seems. Since in all these incarnations of the boy, the novelist describes one common thing—the boy has a deformed thumb. Even Haldar has this deformity. There is neither a physical improvement, nor the intellectual improvement in all these personalities of the boy.

Through these parallel events, the mystery of the plot gets thicker and denser. When one asks the questions of why and in what direction the events lead to, one feels baffled. A mystery novel would have clues that lead to the solution. Here the novelist has wonderfully and vividly created the mysterious happenings and has attempted to relate them, only to arrive at nothingness. At the end, AVA shows Murugan, Urmila and Sonali rushing to the station Sealdah, where they are told Phulboni and Mrs. Arnouin have gone. This is the place from which Murugan has been recorded as missing. Since August 1995 and is not heard of till his ID card appearance on AVA screen. What happens to the rest of them is left to the imagination of the reader. But Sealdah is the station from where Mangala and Laakhan were hired; it is the place that plays vanishing tricks causing most of the characters to disappear. One moment they are all rushing to the station in 1995, with Urmila saying that she would save them and take them across, the next moment we find Antar hearing voices, finding resemblance between Tara and Urmila and Maria and Sonali, talking to him, as if they were all with him in his room, "a voice whispering in his ear, 'keep watching; we're here; we are all with you.'" (256) That is Tara along with the rest of the characters saying, "we'll help you across." (256)

The question is from what he is to be saved and where he has to go across. This mystery with its mysticism remaining almost unexplained and unrelated. Ghosh tries to explain this with his theory of counter-Science and secrecy thereof, and contradictions of knowledge. He mentions the search for the ultimate transcendence of nature, of immortality: "What I'm really talking about is a technology for interpersonal transference" (90), explaining the failure of the body and migration therefrom. This technology he calls the Calcutta chromosome. The oriental belief of life beyond life, birth and rebirths, the novelist attempts to explore. Herein we find the echoes of the *Bhagvad Gita*, about body being a sort of garment to be discarded when it turns old and torn to acquire a new, fresh garment for the soul. The end-result of the application of this theory to the characters in the novel is far from satisfactory. Rushdie-like, Ghosh has picked up the topical issue of the recurrence of the malarial fever, and in the feverish delusion, he has presented a secondary world in space and time, though highly imaginative, yet it very unconvincingly remains unfelt. Sprinkling of metaphysical concepts does not enhance in any way the deeply felt moral or aesthetic convictions. They make the novel readable but do not create an impression of wholeness, of some special perception and experience of the primary world. As Meenakshi Mukherjee remarks: "To prise them out one would have to read the novel a second time."[4] Jaya Banerji consideres it 'far-fetched' and compares it to the grandma's 'Bengali braid,' with the thread of malarial research running through the novel: "If Ghosh ever drew his storyline on a blackboard he would end up with real granny's knot of a plot—each character's life intertwined with the others in some way or the other. As for direction, he proceeds in ever decreasing circles until he comes to the centre which is where he started in the first place."[5]

There are certain passages which are beautiful and vivid especially the Phulboni stories narrated by Urmila and Phulboni's anguished cry for the goddess of silence. Calcutta has been celebrated as the city of joy: portrayed as the voices, and now we have a city craving for the goddess of silence. Is Ghosh too much with too many words: "The word is to silence what the shadow is to the foreshadowed, what the veil is to the eyes, what the mind is to truth, what language is to life." (24) Is it a search for the words of silence? Since the words do not make any sense: "maybe none of this makes sense." (88) Since this is a novel from the author of *The Circle of Reason* (1986) and *The Shadow Lines* (1988), one is tempted to search for the hidden meaning. Instead what we find is something of "an exoticisation of India," to use Meenakshi Mukharjee's words, "How does a writer avoid the allegation of neo-orientalism for such as exoticisation of India?" Against all the inventions and terminology of the new technology, what we find is the characters appearing and disappearing from the screen and life itself without making any impression on the reader's mind as it usually happens with thrillers. Nor do they arrive at any discovery. Shakespeare can best sum up this as "a tale told by an idiot, full of sound and fury, signifying nothing." Is it anything more than "cacoethes scribendi,"[6] disappointing and disillusioning the readers' expectation from Amitav Ghosh?

NOTES

1. (New Delhi: Ravi Dayal, 1996).
2. Malcolm Bradbury, *Possibilities: Essays on the State of the Novel* (London: OUP, 1973).
3. Ann Swinfen, *In Defence of Fantasy* (London: Routledge and Kegan Paul, 1984).
4. Meenakshi Mukherjee, Review in *India To day*, May 15, 1996.
5. Jaya Banerji, Review of *The Calcuta Chromosome* in *Indian Review of Books* Vol. 5, Number 9, June-July 1996, Madras.
6. Editor, *Indian Review of Books*, Vol. 5, number 9, June-July, 1996, Madras.

The Art of Story-Telling: A Study of Vikram Chandra's *Love and Longing in Bombay*

BIJAY KUMAR DAS

The art of story telling is an integral part of Indian literary tradition. Its origin dates back to the sixth century A.D. ancient fables. Old classics like *Katha-Sarit-Sagara, Brihat-Katha* and the *Panchatantra* are famous for the art of story-telling in our country. Stories in the past were written or told (according to the oral tradition) with a bias for morality. They were didactic in nature. Vikram Chandra's *Love and Longing in Bombay* (New Delhi: Penguin India, 1997) marks a departure from the conventional mode of ancient Indian story telling. The five stories in this collection, woven round the classic framing device of an oldman telling stories in a bar, portray contemporary life in India's most sophisticated city of Bombay (recently renamed as Mumbai). The five stories form as it were, an integrated whole and read like a full-length novel.

The first story, "Dharma" is about Major General Jago Antia (real name Jehangir Antia) who returns home in Bombay after being crippled in the war. The narrator of the story, Subramaniam, begins the story with a whispering note: "I knew a man once who met a ghost" and adds, "some people meet their ghosts, and some don't. But we are haunted by them." Jago Antia, as the story unfolds, is haunted by the spirit of a small boy. The story begins on an ominous note: "On the day that Major General Jago Antia turned fifty, his missing leg began to ache." Having resigned his job on medical grounds he came to Bombay, his ancestral place, 'to sell the house.' Amir Khan, the caretaker of the house supported Jago

Antia on this point and urged him: 'Sell it, I'm tired of it.' Tody-walla, to whom Jago Antia wanted to sell it, cried foul: 'there is something in that house.' Jago Antia dismissed it as nonsense and told Thappa, "I will sleep tonight quietly and so will you. No more of this foolishness." As he moved inside the house with Thappa, he heard a voice asking with a sob "where shall I go?"

An exorcist named Thakker came to find out the spirit and he opined that it was a child. He explained: "It is most powerful because it is a child and because it is helpless and because it is alone. Only one who knows it and who is from its family can help it. Such a person must go up there naked and alone. Remember, alone and naked, and ask it what it seeks." (23) Jago Antia went there alone and kicked off his shoes and unbuckled his belt and whispered: "what can you want from me? I was a child too." He went down the memory lane in a flashback and shut his eyes. Chandra uses poetic prose to describe Antia's past and creates a trance-like atmosphere befitting the occasion: "He [Antia] shut his eyes. Somewhere deep came the poisonous seep of memory, he felt it in his stomach like a living stream, and his mother was looking at him, her eyes unfocussed in a kind of daze." (24)

Then we are told about Sohrab, Antia's brother who died young, and Antia's ancestry has been personalized. Haunted by the spirit of the boy, Jago Antia went to the roof and came face to face with it. Chandra depicts the whole scene in a matter-of-fact tone:

> When Jago Antia stirred weakly on the roof, when he looked up, it was dawn. He held himself up and said, "Are you still here? Tell me what you want." Then he saw at the parapet, very dim and shifting in the grey light, the shape of a small body, a boy looking down over the edge towards the ocean. As Jago Antia watched, the boy turned slowly, and in the weak light he saw that the boy was wearing a uniform of olive green, and he asked, "Where shall I go?" Jago Antia began to speak, but then his voice caught, because he was remembering his next and seventh birthday, the first party without Soli, and his parents holding him between them, soothing him, saying you must want something, and he look-

> ing up at their faces, at the lines in his father's face, the exhaustion in his mother's eyes. Burjor Mama sits on the carpet behind him with head down, and Amir Khan stands behind, and Jehangir shakes his head. His mother's eyes fill with tears, and she kisses him on the forehead, "Baba, it's all right, let us give you a present," and his heart breaks beneath a surging weight, but he stands up straight, and looking at her and his father, he says, "I want a uniform." So Jago Antia looked at the boy as he came closer, and he saw the small letters above the pocket, J. ANTIA, and the sun came up, and he saw the enormous dark eyes, and in the eyes he saw his vicious and ravenous strength, his courage and his devotion, his silence and his pain, his whole misshapen and magnificent life, and Jago Antia said, "Jehangir, Jehangir, you're already at home." (30-31)

The story comes to a close with Thappa and Amir Khan offering Jago Antia a cup of tea in order to bring him back to reality. Chandra concludes the story with a note of relief. "'Thank you,' Jago Antia said. Then they drank the tea together."

The second story in this collection, "Shakti," is about two rival business families whose women Sheila Bijlani and Dolly Boatwalla are ill disposed to each other. The club culture of Bombay life with its so-called sophistication is exposed thoroughly in this story. Sheila, a beautiful Air Hostess, married the U.S.A. returned Bijlani (T.T.) for money and started a business. In their neighbourhood lived Dolly Boatwalla in her Boatwalla mansion. There was a Lunch Club in Bombay, dominated by Dolly. Sheila in spite of the former's objection finally succeeded in joining the lunch club. Chandra gives a vivid description of the club: "The women in the Lunch Club met once a month for lunch at one of the members' houses. After lunch they played cards. Then they had tea and went home. That was it, nothing very exciting on the face of it, but if you knew anything you knew that was where marriages were arranged and sometimes destroyed, deals were made, casually business was felt out, talk went on about this minister in Delhi and So-and-So's son who was school captain at Mayo. It was the real stuff, you know, masala-grinding, how the world works." (37)

The Lunch Club met next at Sheila's house for lunch. The dish was served and during the lunch Sheila's son Sanjeev was introduced to the members. Mani Mennon, Sheila's friend, liked the boy. "Isn't he so cute?" Mani said, but Dolly was offensive. Sheila turned and saw 'the look on Dolly's face, a kind of absurd pursing of the nostrils, an unmistakable look of offense, as if she had just begun to smell something bad.' The bitterness between Sheila and Dolly took a new turn. Chandra brings a contrast between the two in a simple but forceful language:

> Dolly was not perfect, she was long everywhere, she was sallow, she wore old jewelry sometimes missing a link here and there, today she wore a tatty green scarf over her shirt, and that was just it. Sheila was perfect, and she knew that however hard she tried she could never achieve the level of careless imperfection that Dolly flaunted. It had nothing to do with perseverance or intelligence and it took generations. It couldn't be learnt, only grown with the bone. It was absolutely confident and sure of itself and easy. Dolly had it and she didn't looking at it honestly, Sheila knew this. She knew it and she was absolutely determined that if it took her the rest of her life she would defeat Dolly that it had come to open conflict she knew, and she would not stand losing. (41-42)

Sheila launched a new club called the Shanghai Club with the help of Mr. Fong. Dolly was invited to join it. The war between Sheila and Dolly continued for a long time. The feud between the two can be taken as a symbol of the conflict between women of the high society who can do anything for the sake of their vanity. False sense of dignity and vulgar display of wealth are taken as a distinguishing mark of new culture in the present-day society. The desire to show up oneself and look down upon others becomes a way of life with the so-called upper class women in the metropolis of our country. No wonder that both Sheila and Dolly fell a prey to this kind of modern malaise and continued their war to the bitter end. Chandra has rightly observed: "Shiela and Dolly had conducted a ruthless but fiercely polite war for years, in which the victories were counted in receptions given and famous writers annexed and huge sums collected for causes and the causalities were bruised egos of partisans of either side, who cut each other in Derby boxes and flicked razor-sharp looks over shoulders at openings. But there were some rulers, a certain code of conduct that kept it all civilized until the incident of the blackball."

The story took a dramatic turn when Sheila's son Sanjeev fell in love with Dolly's third daughter, Roxanne, and expressed his desire before his mother to marry the girl. Sheila was shocked but she kept her cool. Dolly took Roxanne to London. Sanjeev's agony for not being united with Roxanne shattered him and made his mother realize the futility of her feud with Dolly. At Asha's (Ganga's daughter) wedding, Sheila observed that her relatives and Dolly's relatives had gathered under the same Shamiana to bless the newly wed couple, and children of both the families, Roxanne's second cousin and her niece, played there. This made her change her mind. Perhaps, she was willing to make amends by asking Dolly to marry her daughter to Sanjeev. The story ends with a hope, 'Maybe I'll tell you about that another evening.'

Apart from exposing the hollowness of the feud in upper class society and the hypocrisy of high people to whom 'the rest of the world is invisible,' Chandra has made references to living personalities like Amitabh Bachchan and Tiger Pataudi in his effort to create new myths around them. This is certainly a daring act to mythicize the living heroes in the field of art and sports. Raja Rao made such an attempt in *Kanthapura* to create myth around Gandhi, the father of the nation. Chandra has also made references to several films of Amitabh Bachchan like Coolie, Dewar, Sholay and Muqaddar Ka Sikandar. He has also used a lot of Indian words without making an attempt at translation. The success of the story lies in the fact that he has successfully recreated his characters in their own situation.

The third story in the collection, "Kama," dives deep into the intricacies of the life in the city of Bombay and exposes the hypocrisy of the so-called sophisticated people. Police Inspector Sartaj Singh while investing into the murder case of Chetanbhai Ghanshyam Patel gets drawn into the 'spiralling layers of corruption and deceit' prevalent in the society. As the irony of fate would have it, he also reflects upon his discontented married life that ultimately terminates in divorce. In course of investigation, he got pressurized by senior officers like Parulkar and local M.L.A. Shantilal Nayak not to pursue the case too far. "These are delicate times," said Praulkar. "Pushing too hard, without sufficient reason, on that family could lead to, let us say, sensitivities." (110) Sartaj Singh arrested a man called Ghorpada, who not only died in detention but proved to be not guilty in the end. Kshitiji, Patel's son, seemed to be innocent in the beginning but in the end turned out to be a member of an association which is given to violence and lawlessness. The members of the association called themselves 'Rakshaks.' The murdered man, Patel, had connection with a racket that used to exploit women sexually and run a flesh trade. After sex act, nude photographs were taken for blackmail afterwards. What is worse, he has not spared his own wife, Ashaben. Chandra makes reference to several people who were given to crime, sex and failed in love.

Sartaj Singh, the investigating police officer, was also a victim of failed married life. His wife, Megha, who married him for love in their college days, decided to marry someone called Raj Sanghi. The worse is that Megha came personally to Sartaj to inform him about her decision, "I am getting married." (116) What is most surprising is that the wife (Megha) who came to inform the husband (Sartaj) of her decision to marry Raj enters into an elaborate sex act for hours together and Vikram Chandra takes nearly ten pages (116-25) to describe the love-play between them:

> He felt Megha's hands on his shoulders, and her breath on his forehead as she whispered, "Sartaj, Sartaj," and he turned away from her. From his own embarrassment, but his strength was gone, and she pulled his head back, into the solid curve of her shoulder. He shook again and she held him tight, hard, and he felt with piercing awareness the pain of her forearm against the back of his neck. He was gone, then, vanished into the familiar fragrance of her perfume, unknown for so long, with its flowers and underlying tinge of salt. He was perfectly still. Her lips moved against his cheek, murmuring, something that he couldn't quite hear, and then he felt the brush on his mouth, a gift of softness and then the shifting

> suppleness, what he always experienced as a question. He kissed her desperately, afraid to stop or pause because then she would stop. But she wasn't stopping, she held his face in her hands, her long palms strongly on cheeks and chin, and sipped at him with little murmurs. Despite himself, Sartaj curved against her, an arm up and around, and he felt the weight of her breasts against his side, and she laughed into his mouth, not here, not here. (118)

The scene, then shifts to the bed room.

> Finally she drew him up and kissed him, licking his mouth and fingers. This time he put the condom on himself. They moved together and the bed creaked under them. His body bent over her and he looked back over his shoulder at their tangled shadows, rising and falling, and then down at her and at their hair mingling. He bent down to kiss her, and when he came away she was crying. With a groan he touched her cheek but she put a hand on his wrist. "Don't stop," she said. "Don't stop. Don't stop." And so he went on. In the twilight she raised a hand to his mouth and he could see her tears. And so then a moment when everything was lost, but her. (124-25)

Sartaj's own married life, (rather the failure of it) made him understand the murdered Patel's wedded life, who did everything for money and pleasure and, "under his hands there was Chetanbhai's case file, closed. It was over, according to the file, and there was a murderer who had died in the hospital." (159)

The story comes to an end not only with the closure of the murder case but with Sartaj's divorce of his wife, Megha. The wheel has turned a full circle. Chandra does not offer solutions to the problems presented in the story. There are only hints and guesses, and it is for the discerning readers to read meanings into it.

The fourth story in the collection, "Artha," is about gangsters. Here the narrator, Subramaniam, tells us a story told to him by a stranger on the Rajdhani train, when the former was travelling from Delhi to Bombay. The main characters in the story are two—

Sandhya and the protagonist, Iqbal Akbar, but other minor characters are Anubhav (the painter with whom Sandhya is in love), Latif (Sandhya's son), Vasant (Sandhya's ex-husband), Ratmani (a builder), Rajesh (Iqbal's friend, the missing postal clerk) and a few others. Rajesh and Iqbal met Anubhav in Sandhya's house. At that time Anubhav was painting something against the backdrop of Amitabh Bachchan in Coolie's rope in his film Deewar. Gradually the story unfolds that Sandhya has a son, an ex-husband and a mother. She is drawn towards Anubhav who works for the *Times of India.* Iqbal saw them 'standing nearby with their heads close together.'

As the story proceeds, we are told that Rajesh, who worked in the post office, was missing. Iqbal searched for him and in the process encountered the gangsters, the underworld people and was beaten by them. The 'bhai log' (the underworld people whose leader was Govardhan Bhai) played tricks on Iqbal. Iqbal describes in a matter-of-fact tone a scene in the underworld when he was tortured by them: "When I managed to focus my eyes I saw three uniformed guards with lathis in their hands standing over me. To the left there was a man in plain clothes, with hair cut short and a very straight back. In his hands he held a sten gun, the muzzle pointed directly at me. And stepping through the gate there was the man with the clipped moustache from the Atreya Lane gym." (209)

The story has reference to a communal riot which created havoc. People belonging to different communities who lived together for ages turned enemies in no time. Iqbal came to know that Rajesh worked with some 'bhai log' and one of them was Ratmani. Iqbal lost a friend, Rajesh, to the people of the underworld. The sub-inspector's cryptic reply, "in this life some people just vanish," explains the deplorable state of life in the modern metropolis. Painting turns out to be more lively than life. Iqbal concludes the story by imagining what Rajesh would look like in a painting (because Rajesh the person is lost for ever): "I will lie in my long narrow room and look at the strong fingers holding the white cigarette and wonder what it is in the shapes that is Rajesh." (228)

The last story in this collection, "Shanti," is written in a different vein. It is here that the teller enters the tale and the story gets a personal touch. Subramaniam, the teller of the stories, invites the narrator to his house to say how he met Shanti and married her. Characters in his story are very few but they are convincing as human beings. Frankil Furtado, the assistant station master at Leharia, puts Mrs. Shanti Chauhan, a second class passenger in first class because 'she is very beautiful.' Frankie has taken interest in Shanti, as she used to come to that station every two or three months. When Subramaniam asked him about Shanti's destination, "Going where?" Frankie replied, "I don't know. She catches a tonga outside the station. I think to the cantonment. Her attache has stencilling on it." (237) She is a married woman who is in search of her missing pilot husband. On being asked about her husband, she said: "He was in the first batch of Indian fighter pilots in the RIAF. He was flying a Hurricane over Burma in 1942. They were protecting transports. They were attacked by Japanese fighters. The last his wingman saw of him was the plane losing height over the jungle. The plane was smoking. That was all they saw." (243)

She was hopeful of her husband's return but gradually the hope receded. In the meanwhile Shiv Subramaniam took interest in her and tried to win her over. At this point, the author introduces a story-within-the-story and makes Shanti tell the stories to Subramaniam. She told him how she met the man with the bluest eyes, who was also the 'most evil man in the world.' Then she told another story about Zingu who died because he thought 'all men are equal' and asked for equality of status with other upper caste people. For showing this kind of courage, he was killed along with his son. Then Shanti told stories about ghosts as to how they had cast their spell on Janamohini and made us aware of nuclear warfare as it affected Amma. These stories are told to build a kind of intimacy between Shiv and Shanti. At long last Shiv proposed to Shanti which she accepted and happily they became man and wife. The story comes to a close with the narrator being introduced to Shanti, Subramaniam's wife. The fitting conclusion to the series of five stories comes when the narrator feels like asking Ayesha to marry him, so that they can get into life. The narrator concludes the story with an assertion of life. "I know I am looking for Ayesha. I will stand before her building and when it is morning I will call up to her. I might ask her to go for a walk. I might ask her to marry me. If we search together, I think, we may find in Andheri, in Colaba, in Bhuleshwar, perhaps not heaven or its opposite, but only life itself." (267-68)

In *Love and Longing in Bombay*, Vikram Chandra has adopoted a new technique of story telling. The five stories in this collection are told by the same person and are interlocked with a dozen of shorter narratives, fused together as it were, by a 'story-within-the-story' technique. To read these stories is to see Bombay inside out. Violence, crime, activities in the underworld, club-culture, witch-hunting—all the negative qualities that dehumanize the modern man are highlighted in these stories with consummate skill. What seems to me to be more important in this collection of stories, is the use of Indian words by way of code mixing, that successfully recreates, the characters in our own situation. The use of Indian words like 'thali,' 'diya,' 'massala,' 'dupatta,' 'shamiana,' jira,' 'paan,' 'bidis,' 'maidan,' 'akhara,' 'bas,' 'tap-tap,' 'tamasha,' 'daroga,' 'dusserimango,' 'besan,' 'Karhais,' 'bhajiyas,' 'puris,' 'haveli,' 'takath,' 'durbans,' 'safas,' 'pranam,' 'rakshaks,' 'kurta,' 'pyjamas,' 'panchnama,' 'agarbattis,' 'saukeen,' 'regada-patis,' 'patta,' 'peripauna,' 'jite raho beta,' 'janaab,' 'kaisehai,' '(pati) parameswar' and swear words like 'bhenchod,' 'maderchod,' 'dada,' 'bewda,' 'kalua,' 'musalta,' 'kattu,' etc. evokes an atmosphere in which the characters live and interact with each other. Apart from using Indian words in his attempt at creating an Indian English idiom, Chandra also takes recourse to transliteration to recreate a familiar scene in his stories. Here are a few examples:

i) Maine Shayad tumhe pahale bhi kahin dekha hai. (26)
ii) Voh jo ham me tum me karaar tha, tumhe yaad ho ke na yaad ho. (104)
iii) Baat karni mujhe kabhi muskil aisi to na thi. (105)
iv) Stop Phenko-ing, yaar. (163)
v) Dandi mein current hai? (198)

Love and Longing in Bombay depicts the "horror and boredom" of the city of Bombay in our time. The book successfully fictionalizes some aspects of modern life in our metropolis and makes an absorbing reading.

Gulzar's *Raavi Paar and Other Stories*: A Valuable Contribution to Partition Literature

ALKA SAXENA

In 1947 the northern part of a great empire became a blazing inferno. Terror-stricken people either died or had a close encounter with death. The catastrophe seemed to bring everything to an end. Amidst destruction, the year 1947 also saw the creation of Pakistan and Independent India. From the historical point of view, a new star rose in the east. Colourful ceremonies marked the birth of a nation. But for the common man the bitterness and agony of Partition was unbearable. The year 1998 has been of great significance for Indians. It marks the golden jubilee of India's Independence. Once again such calculations are for historical and political purposes. For the common man the bitterness and agony of 1947 is a wound that still hurts.

Recent trends of writing in the subcontinent show that the subject matter and theme of poets and authors has been the trauma of Partition. The haunting memories of the horrific butchering both in India and Pakistan lie at the very core of some recently published short stories and novels. Urvashi Butalia's chilling exploration of Partition memories in *The Other Side of Silence: Voices from the Partition of India* leaves readers with a sense of numbness. Flashes of horror mark *An Epic Unwritten: Partition Stories* edited by Mohd. Umar Memon. Memoirs of loss and a search for personal space are recorded in Ajeet Caur's *Pebbles in a Tin Drum*. The agony and ecstasy of the Partition is so sensitively portrayed in Shiv K. Kumar's *A River with Three Banks*. Qurratulain Hyder's *River of Fire*, an English translation of her landmark work *Aag Ka Darya* is one of the most powerful tomes about the deranged days of Partition. To this genre of publication belongs Gulzar's *Raavi Paar and Other Stories*. A study of these stories of Partition poignantly conveys that fifty years down the line, the schisms have only deepened.

Gulzar's collection of short stories has a distinct cameo quality, which is reflected in the subject-matter and style. Those tumultuous times continue to haunt him even today. The trauma and pain comes alive in this collection of short stories. Gulzar admits, "what I have felt from within, I have written and presented to you." It appears that after all these years Gulzar has finally mustered the courage to start exorcising all those evil forces and demons. The stories in this collection are by turns serious, moving, funny and ironic. They have been written by an unconventional story-teller, whose gifts of a photographic memory and creative imagination manifest themselves in revealing the truth and reality of existence with sincerity and sensitivity.

Gulzar was born in Deena (now in Pakistan) in 1936 and after Partition he came to Delhi. Yet even today when he talks of what he left behind, it is with great melancholy and pain. In the Foreword to *Raavi Paar and Other Stories*, he writes: "I had witnessed the partition of India from very close quarters in 1947. It left me bruised and scarred. I cannot help but write about this excruciating period. I wrote the short stories with the background of the partition to try and get the painful experience out of my system. On sharing them with my readers, I hope very much to distance myself from the stories. My only wish that these stories do not re-ignite the latent anguish once again, in some reader who witnessed the gory partition with his own eyes."[1] The very fact that Gulzar feels the need to get the painful experience out of his system bears testimony to the severity of the damage caused to his psyche—his soul. Even after fifty years, the anguish exists. The deep sense of insecurity and loss have become a part of his system. Probably with the recent outbreak of riots in Bombay and several other parts of India, the same old fear, the "khauf" has resurfaced.

"Khauf" is the title of the first story in this collection. It is set in riot-torn Bombay. There had been riots in the city for the last four days. Yasin had been away for four days. He was waiting at the platform to board a local train. When the train appeared, he was unable to decide which compartment he should enter—as the majority of passengers were Hindus. He, therefore, chose an empty compartment. But when he realized that there was another man in it, his first reaction was that this man was certainly a Hindu. The bakery where Yasin worked was set on fire when the riots had broken suddenly. As he tried to run away in order to save his life, he was caught by Bhau, a Hindu, who provided him shelter in his own room. Bhau knew that Yasin was a Muslim. But he was also aware of the mentality and attitude of the blood and fire; so he made Yasin wear his sacred thread and kept him in his room for four days. Yasin was naturally worried about his family and when the curfew was lifted for a few hours, he went to Andheri station to board a local train. When he saw the man in the compartment, "His nerves were on edge with fear. As he sat his knees shook so much it seemed as if he was about to have an epileptic fit." (1) Fear gripped Yasin and he felt cold sweat trickle down his face out of sheer terror. From his hiding place Yasin observed that the man had closed all the doors of the compartment. He felt as if all routes of escape were being closed. "He reached the extreme edge of fear: he was being trapped in a cave." (6) When he felt that there was no chance of his escape, he suddenly gathered all his strength and shouted "Ya Ali" as he grabbed the man's legs and threw him out. As the man fell off the train, Yasin heard him scream "Allah. . . ." Yasin was shocked to know that the man was a Muslim too. Although he felt sorry, "But having freed himself from the noose of terror he felt as if he had escaped from the jaws of death." (7) Yasin had managed to save his life and ultimately reached his family, his home. Flaring up of communal riots and the mob frenzy spell disaster for innocent victims like Yasin. After a close encounter with death, a fresh lease of life was given but what is significant is that the Khauf always remains. The bitter memories may fade but never die.

"Sometimes life runs leaping like a wounded cheetah, and leaves the claw marks here and there. If you connect these marks you will see a strange pattern." (57) These are the opening lines of the story titled "Batwara." It is the story of an old Punjabi named Sardar Harbhajan Singh, who firmly believed that Gulzar, the author, was his youngest son whom he had lost during the riots that broke at the time of Partition in 1947. At that time he had also lost his daughter, but, by the grace of God he managed to find her after thirty years. The Sardar told Gulzar how and when they had lost him. He still remembered the terrible riots, the flames and fire. Even at that time he pretended to put up a brave front but inwardly they all were terrified. He confessed to Gulzar, "To tell you the truth Sampooran kaka, our faith had been shattered, our roots had been shaken." (63) When it became too unsafe to live there, they decided to pick up a few things and escape. Often during the tedious journey the parents lost sight of their children and "called out to them in anguished despair." (63) One dark night when the caravan was at Mianwali gali the rumour spread that a Muslim mob would be attacking them. While narrating this particularly sensitive incident the Sardar fell silent for a while. His eyes were moist and very quietly he managed to say, "It was during that night that we lost both our youngest children." (64) The Sardar was sure that Gulzar was none other than his son Sampooran Singh. Even the wife of the Sardar aired similar feelings "Punni [Sampooran] why don't you believe us. Why do you want to hide from us? You have changed your name to Gulzar. Just as Satya's name was changed to Dilshad." (67) Gulzar repeated the history of his family and left the couple feeling hopeless. Incidentally Gulzar's real name happens to be Sampooran Singh. Eight years after this incident, in 1993, Gulzar received a letter from the Sardar's elder son Iqbal. Along with the letter was a card for a Bhog ceremony announcing that Sardar Harbhajan Singh had passed away. Iqbal had written to Gulzar because his mother wanted him to inform her youngest son about his father's death. As Gulzar read the letter from Iqbal, he felt as if his own father, his Darji, had passed away. The eternal hope of meeting long lost family members is not that of Darji alone. Such hopes keep fluttering in the deep recesses of the broken hearts of many fathers, brothers, mothers, sisters, husbands—the list is endless.

The title story "Raavi Paar" is the most poignant and touching of all the stories in this collection. Probably Darshan Singh, the protagonist of this sad tale, also hopes like Darji that his son may still be alive. "Raavi Paar" is the story of a Sikh couple who has been blessed with twins. Darshan Singh's wife Shahni had delivered twins in the Gurudwara, where Hindus and Sikhs had secretly begun to gather as riots spread in Lyalpur. The twins were born on Sankranti, an auspicious day, but the same night the whole family, along with many other refugees had to flee Pakistan on the roof of a train. "One of the twins was very weak and there was very little hope of his survival but Shahni had struggled to keep him alive." (45) Although she was very weak, yet she consented to leave the Gurudwara and join the caravan of refugees for the sake of her sons. Darshan Singh placed his children in a wicker basket and lifted it onto his head. When they reached the station, the train was there but there was no free space in it. "People seemed to sprout from the roofs of the compartment like grass." (45) Amidst this stress and strain the exhausted mother tried to "suckle each child alternately from breasts that had seen sucked dry." (45) As the train puffed in the darkness, Darshan Singh noticed that one child was very still. When he touched the child he found to his dismay that he was cold and had been dead for some time. Darshan Singh wailed loudly, the people around him tried to take the dead child from Shahni, "but she sat like a statue, and clutched the basket to her chest." (46) When the train reached Lahore, someone suggested to Darshan Singh that he should throw the dead child in the river Raavi rather than carry him to the other side. Darshan Singh cautiously pulled the basket away and in a purgatorial gesture, he threw the child into the river, exclaiming 'Wahe Guru.' It was only when he heard the scream that he realized he had sacrificed not the dead but the living child into the river, that was supposed to separate past from present. "Darshan Singh looked in terror towards his wife. She was clutching the dead child to her chest." It is a chilling metaphor for Gulzar's own childhood trauma and he says: "It is I who have been left behind and drowned, it is I who have come this side."[2]

In the story "Raavi Paar," Darshan Singh was left with the empty wicker basket. Partition had earlier snatched his father and in the end his twins are also lost. He had reached the other side, the safe side—but now the whole exercise, taking shelter in the Gurudwara, leaving Beeji behind, undertaking the risky journey have been futile. The narration of the story no doubt ends, but the remarks of Gulzar show that the trauma of real life Darshan Singhs cannot. The feelings of loss, incompleteness, something missing, always haunt the survivor.

Nothingness, the sense of having lost all in life, is the central theme of the story "Jamun Ka Per." The atmosphere of this story is also surcharged with the frenzy of Partition. "The sturdy, outstretched branches of the Jamun tree rested on the two buildings like the protective arms of a father. The tree in whose lap innumerable children had been nurtured to grow into fine youngmen, and in whose shade the elderly found refuge from the trials and travails of life, was the axis of that entire neighbourhood." (161) For the villagers the main object was to throw the British out first. Jaichand, Sardarji, Lala Lekhraj all agreed that "other things could be taken care of afterwards. After all we are all brothers. We can set the things amongst ourselves even if we quarrel." (158) But came 1947 and communal riots broke out. Fire ignited at Sadar Bazar, Paharganj and upto the Subzi Mandi. The flag of the Muslim League and the tricolour which were hoisted on different branches of the Jamun tree "crashed against each other and landed on the ground along with the branches. The two arms of the patriarch were chopped off followed by his sons digging their nails into each other's breasts like maniacs. Blood squirted in streams and spattered across the father's face." (162) The humiliation during the colonial rule was no doubt disgusting. But then the atrocities were committed by the Britishers—they were foreigners. But in 1947 there were communal riots and at that time friends turned into foes. The feeling of brotherhood among Hindu, Muslims and Sikhs seemed to burn in the flames that spread everywhere with a vengeance. The branches of the Jamun tree were chopped off to keep the pyres of innocent riot victims burning. The author's heart is filled with grief when he says that now when he looks at the Jamun tree his heart aches with a hollow feeling. Ultimately all is lost in despair. "With its shade having been taken away from the Jamun tree, there is nothing left. Nothing." (63) This last sentence of the story highlights the emptiness and hollowness that came in 1947 and the memories of loss are still fresh in the aggrieved souls of the survivors.

Millions of people were displaced during Partition. People had believed that Partition would mean different government on both sides of the divide, but they never imagined even in their wildest dreams that millions of people would be driven out from their ancestral homes to unknown destinations. Urvashi Butalia's *The Other Side of Silence: Voices from the Partition of India* is a deeply sensitizing contribution to partition literature. The author describes it as a "minuscule effort to uncover the less explored human dimensions of the history of Partition."[3] The interviews in the book remain etched in memory. During the course of several interviews she took for the book, it became clear to Butalia that "it was really important to excavate these memories so that you could see that the picture is much more complex. Also, in order to forget you have to remember. Only then you could put it behind you and genuinely forget."[3] A parallel pattern is reflected in Gulzar's creativity.

But even if all is lost, Gulzar sees hope in man's ability to transcend man-made boundaries. After Partition the border between India and Pakistan had been clearly marked and defined. Except for the extremists on either side of the dividing line, the people in general feel that "no system had yet been devised to seal the borders of thought."[4] Many people will nod in agreement with Gulzar's optimistic statement: "Just as India is divided into different states yet remains unified, the people of India and Pakistan are essentially the same. We will cross man-made borders one day because ultimately we are looking towards unity."[1] *Raavi Paar and Other Stories* has familiarized the people with another facet of celluloid poet Gulzar's talents. The world of pain and conflict has been resolved with gentle Gulzarian grace and note of optimism.

NOTES

1. (New Delhi: Harper Collins, 1997).
2. *India Today*, 27 Oct. 1997, p. 101.
3. Sakina Yusuf Khan, "Encounter," Interview with Urvashi Butalia, *The Times of India*, 31 August 1998, p. 6.
4. *So That You Can Know Me, An Anthology of Pakistani Women Writers*, ed. Yasmin Hameed and Asif Ali Farrukhi (New Delhi: Harper Collins, 1997), p. 144.

Ethel Wilson's *Swamp Angel* and Shashi Deshpande's *The Binding Vine* as Kunstlerroman

S. INDIRA

"Quest" an important element in myth, in fiction and in life is especially prominent in Kunstlerroman, a genre that deals with formation, development and problems of the artist. As a critic claims, "in the twentieth century Kunstlerroman, the theme of the quest for identity is intimately connected with the concept of the discovery of self through the process of creation so that the actual creation of work has become the subject of many contemporary artist-novels."[1] Sylvia Plath's *The Bell Jar*, Willa Cather's *The Song of the Lark*, Dorothy Richardson's *Pilgrimage* serve as examples of Kunstlerroman written about women artists operating under the psychological and sociological burdens of a patriarchal society and its myths.

Ethel Wilson's *Swamp Angel* (1954) and Shashi Deshpande's *The Binding Vine* (1992) fall into this genre as both novels portray the conflicts of their artist-protagonists between life and art and between the woman and the artist "two mutually exclusive things at one and the same time."[2] Divided as they are, by the need to create and the need to love, they face the dual dilemma, unable to strike a balance between the woman in them who is supposed to be passive, weak and self-less as dictated by the patriarchal set up and the artist-self which desires freedom from the demands of life, seeks and strives to gain personal fulfilment in experience.

Ethel Wilson's novels occupy an anomalous place in Canadian literature as she has dealt with the theme of a woman's search for freedom and independence—a lonely quest for self-discovery—a theme foreign to Canadian writing in the 1940s and 50s. Shashi Deshpande's novels too show women concerned with the complex and difficult social and psychological problem of defining an authentic self. While Wilson's heroines seek to establish a link with the larger human community being deprived of an intimate bond of family, Deshpande's women protagonists search for their individual fulfilment within the orbit of family due to an inalienable bond to tradition.

Swamp Angel,[3] considered to be Ethel Wilson's master work, traces the struggle of its artist-heroines in the suffocating web of patriarchy in order to be free, independent and fulfilled. The title *Swamp Angel* refers to a gun which has a historical origin, being used in a battle fought to prevent the abolition of slavery. It is the central symbol of the novel signifying the non-conformity of Ethel Wilson, a brilliant circus-performer, who used to juggle with revolvers like Swamp Angel, rejecting the mythic image of woman—"The Eternal Feminine." The art of jugglery which has gained for her powers as well as fame has also crippled her role as a woman and mother. As a true artist, she lived a full, intense life, travelling all over the globe in the company of her soul-mate Philip. But she has to endure the contempt of Philip's parents who could not accept "the girl from the circus: into their respectable family, and the anguish of her own parents who were pained to see her leading a hard, vagabond life with Philip who disapproves of the "bonds" of matrimony. Her unconventional life-style and strange, unwomanly profession have distanced her not only from society but also from her daughter Hilda, who is torn between filial devotion and resentment. The Swamp Angel, the habitual companion of her mother is always a painful reminder to Hilda, of her mother's success and her own unlighted childhood when she was an object of constant ridicule and mockery. Yet, she tolerates its presence and place in her mother's life as a unique gift to Nel, whose pleasure and pride would be irrevocably destroyed if she were to know the truth.

On the other hand, Nel is aware that she has failed Hilda as a mother. Looking at the stern, unhappy face of her daughter, she suffers from guilt and remorse. She begins to feel that perhaps it is not fair that she has had everything, "all the fun, glamour, power and Philip" (65) and apologizes to Hilda that she could not change her ways as they were 'set' by the time the girl was born. As she confesses to Maggie later, "But with me, it was Philip or Hilda, I know I was in the web, I did the best I could in the web and it takes God himself to be fair to two different people at once." (151)

While she was "belle laide with a funny tongue" (65) to Philip, with whom she could be absolutely free and uninhibited, she always had to be on guard with Hilda, who gets galled easily. Hilda's love for her mother is overshadowed by her fear of being cowed down by her wise, powerful mother who can look on world and men with an ironical and amused detachment. After her success with Edward Vardoe, Maggie's second husband, Hilda feels "People should not be so powerful, people should not always succeed." (49) This daily conflict between mother and daughter gets resolved by Nell's decision to send away the "Angel" to Maggie. She is forced to abandon the gun which is her "life" now, in order to avoid a possible scandal which would infuriate Hilda, as the gun attracted the attention of the curious neighbourhood during an accident. The act of Nell assumes a symbolic significance as it established Maggie as her true "spiritual heir," glorifying her inner strength and resolve to lead an authentic life and also releases Hilda from her obsessive complexes and painful memories. Hilda flowers into a normal human being, her coldness melting into tenderness and her mistrust fading away letting her to commit herself to love. By clearing all the obstacles, first the gun, then her own domineering self, Nell paves the way for Hilda to get married to the man she loves and live happily as a loving wife and doting mother, the conventional roles she enjoys playing in a subconscious retaliation against her mother's totally unconventional life.

Maggie Lloyd, the strong, quiet woman who can make excellent, artistic files and signboards, who can manage a fishing-lodge efficiently, who can create a pleasant, comfortable assuring environment (The art of making atmospheres—as big an art as any other, says Mariam in Dorothy Richardson's *Pilgrimage*) who can gain the trust and love of people around her is the second artist-heroine of *Swamp Angel.* The novel begins with her escape from her second marriage, a period of "slavery" and nightly humiliation (13) into a wider world. Her serene joy is manifest in the way she sits "gloriously alone," in the back seat of the car, exulting in each small sight and sound in "new time," in "new space" (23) feeling as if she had just been born. (34) The three days she spends at the Simikameen cabins, amidst nature, absorbing into her every pore, the laughing river, the sombrenes and denseness of the forests in a state of pure enchantment and ecstasy, are like the respite that comes to the soul after death. (37) Her spirit thus rejuvenated, Maggie begins her journey through the village of "Hope" to be her own "self" and to realize her potential. Drawn by the strange beauty of the countryside which stirs her poetic imagination, she takes up the job of a cook in a fishing lodge at Three Loon Lake. The beauty and serenity of the place, the lake hidden behind rows of pine trees, away from the hubbub of human inhabitation enchants Maggie and she feels she has arrived at her destination. *Three Loon Lake* thus becomes the symbol of Maggie's quest. The more she identifies herself with the place, with an intuitive affinity and sense of belonging, the more she becomes the focus of Vera's jealousy. Vera's resentment against the lake, its place in her husband's life has thus extended to Maggie, who has given a new lease of life to the crumbling lodge. Unable to bear her success and popularity, not only with the guests at the lodge but also with her husband, Haldar and son, Alan, who simply dote on her, Vera hurts the otherwise "unhurtable" (89) Maggie with her venomous diatribes. Maggie, preferring to be a powerful "swimmer," (90) shakes off her anger and bitterness by deciding to swim past obstacles like Vera: "Swimming is like living, it is done alone." (99) Sometimes, out of sheer weariness with the complex web of human relationships, she wishes to be a seal or a porpoise as "they have a nice life, lived in the cool water with fun and passion without human relation." (100) But her artist-self reasserts itself insisting on finding its fulfilment not in passive self-sacrifice but in active, vital self-realization. The great northern lights declaiming lavishly and fading with indifference as if to say "I may come back but only if I choose, I do as I wish, I am powerful. I am gone but I am here" (96) personify Maggie's determined self. Her life is no longer stagnant as she has moved forward and found her place with other people again, serving them, humouring them and making her way on her own. She is not going to be on the run again as she had done earlier once on losing her father, her husband and daughter and again on being forced to forsake her independence. She realizes the strength and indestructibility of family however maddening it sometimes can be. Deeply concerned about the future of the Chinese boy, Alan, Haldar and the lake itself, as they have become her family now, Maggie decides to cope with the folly of the unhappy Vera (house-bound Vera without an opening window). (52) Her decision is symbolically conveyed in her throwing the "Swamp Angel," up in the air, higher than Nell had ever attempted, giving it a decent farewell yet relinquishing the power and freedom it symbolizes, in order to be part of the human community. As Nell realizes in the later part of her life that one has to be involved in mankind and can't be preoccupied with oneself throughout life, Maggie too comes to see that she can't be immune to human society, forever. And yet, as Maggie writes to Nell, their ability to throw away the substance, to lose all yet keep the essence is very important (129) as they are artists as well as human beings.

In contrast to *Swamp Angel*, where the artist-heroines could realize their inner potential despite social barriers, *The Binding Vine*[4] placed in the Indian context, rooted in a rigid patriarchy, presents a different picture. Mira, the young poet, is not as fortunate as Nell Severance, as her artist-self is being stifled for not being able to emerge in the roles society offers her. In a society where a girl has to be extinct as a person, Mira's longing to be known as a poet, to affirm her identity doesn't seem to have a chance of getting realized. "Huddled in my cocoon, a somnolent silkworm will I emerge a beauteous being? Or will I, suffocating, cease to exist?" (65)

Her marriage in which she has no choice is only "a dark-clouded, engulfing night" (66) she awaits with dread. She hates the word "love" as it is uttered by her husband all the time as she knows, his is only a physical obsession. Her body no longer her own, she clings desperately to her inner "self" and doesn't allow him to drag it too. As she seeks a productive solitude, exalting art above life, trying to "do" rather than to "be," she is considered a freak by her husband's family, as her attempts are antithetical to the concept of womanhood. "They called me mad, they, who cocooned themselves in brisly blankets and thought themselves warm when I spoke of my soul that boiled and seethed." (100) Mira's contempt and agony sound very much like Monisha's protest against her husband's family who lead "indoor lives" in Anita Desai's *Voices in the City.*

It is the artist-self in her that perhaps gives her the courage to withstand the thrust of a new name, Nirmala, and a new identity as a wife, on her and to proclaim: "I am Mira." (101) It reminds one of Nell who recounts her distant triumphs to her daughter again and again as if to affirm, "I, the girl, lived." (64) Appalled at her mother's total passivity and resignation even as a child, Mira decides that she would never give away her life dismissing it as nothing. So her will rises like a "monster child," opposing her mother's advice, "never utter a 'no,' submit and your life will be a paradise" (83) and struggles against the man who tries to possess her despite her intense revulsion. The "monster child" is a striking image as it confirms that "when the female artist tries during her journey to the interior to create the myth of the artist as heroine, she usually miscarries, aborts or gives birth to a monster"[5] as this new myth would be totally unacceptable to society.

Like Nell, who abhors wearing hats and feathers and other feminine trinkets, Mira too is burdened with her femininity. (The woman's body is a constant reminder to the artist-heroines of their war against the social constructs that restrict them as artists.[6]) The silver toe-rings and anklets make her stumble and fall. In spite of her fierce denial to be modelled as her mother, Mira realizes she is trapped with no escape routes.

> Whose face is this I see in this mirror
> Unsmiling, grave, bedewed with fear?
> The daughter? No, mother, I am now your shadow. (126)

Yet, just as Nell exhorts Maggie to realize the futility of escape and remaining aloof which had characterized their lives and the inevitability of involvement, it is through Mira's poetry, Urmila realizes that human relationships, always imperfect, survive on hope.

> Tiny fish swimming in the Ocean of my womb
> My body thrills to you;

Bridging the two worlds, you awaken in me
a desire for life
Desire, says the Buddha, is the cause of grief;
but how escape this cord
this binding vine of love?
Fear lies coiled within this
this womb-piercing joy. (136-37)

The anticipatory joy of giving birth to her child though he is the product of a loveless marriage fills Mira as it is her creation just like her favourite poem. At the same time, the fear that this child would make her vulnerable and that she would have to bear the burden of conflict forever if the child happens to be a daughter makes her wish for a male child.

I feel the quickening in my womb,
he moves—why do I call the child, he? (149)

Trying to understand the dichotomy in Mira's life as well as in her writing (her diaries are in English and her creative writing in Kannada), Urmila senses a message being deciphered like a message tapped on the wall by the prisoner in the next cell. Reconstructing the tragic tale of Mira, who dies in childbirth, in order to get a clue to her son Kishore's aloofness as he is now her husband and also to an understanding of chaotic human relationships, Urmila's unvoiced agony gets relieved.

Kalpana, another victim of physical abuse like Mira, Shakutai, the mother who is torn between the fear of scandal that would jeopardize the whole family and anguish for her wronged daughter, Inni, her own mother who suffers from a life-long guilt of having abandoned her daughter in an old crumbling house with the grandparents as she could not convince her husband that she could be a dutiful mother, Vanaa and her daughter with their daily confrontations as the little girl accuses her mother of not being a true mother as she divides her time between her work and her role as a mother, Preeti, with her self-deception and illusions, Baiaji, her loving grandmother who can be cruel to her husband's second family—a large canvas of characters caught in the web of life, victims of circumstances, of uncompromising and unforgiving social mores, of ego clashes deepen Urmila's perceptions regarding the complex, fragile human relations.

Urmila, being a free, independent intellectual, has acquired "a status personality" as a formidable woman, a complex female and a bossy female (25) like Nell Severance. In translating Mira's poems and deciphering her messages, she is trying to come to terms with the dichotomy in each person, in each relationship between love and hate, concern and cruelty, conformity and rebellion. Accepting life's worth despite its many betrayals (she has lost her little daughter Anu) and conflicts, the power of human ties despite their burdensome nature, Urmila regains her courage, and asserts like Maggie, "I'm not going to break," (19) "I am in full control of myself" (20) and looks forward to a continuation of life with her husband and son hoping to bridge the divide in her.

Urmila thus creates a new myth in depicting herself as an artist who is both courageous and womanly. She is not the "monster child" born out of ambivalences but an integrated human being, who can create art without sacrificing her womanhood and without feeling guilty.

NOTES

1. Yerad Jay Yoldberg, "The Artist-Novel in Transition," *English Fiction in Transition*, 4 (1961), pp. 12-27.
2. Sylvia Plath, *The Bell Jar* (1963; rpt. New York: Harper & Row, 1971).
3. Ethel Wilson, *Swamp Angel* (Toronto: McClelland and Stewart, 1954).
4. Shashi Deshpande, *The Binding Vine* (Penguin India, 1992).
5. Grace Steward, *A New Mythos: The Novel of the Artist as Heroine*, p. 177.
6. *Ibid*, p. 179.

In the Name of the Mother: A Feminist Reading of Githa Hariharan's *The Thousand Faces of Night* and Indrani Aikath Gyaltsen's *Daughters of the House*

SRILATA RAVI

It has been customary for feminist criticism to be characterized more in terms of a personal response and less in terms of a definite analytical method. The study of the image of women as it appears in works of male authors nearly always used to be and often still remains a well defined and oft practised critical study. However in the last twenty odd years, clear critical approaches have come to define feminist criticism.[1] This study aims to examine the concept of motherhood portrayed in two recent works of Indian women's fiction in English, *The Thousand Faces of Night* by Githa Hariharan[2] and *Daughters of the House* by Indrani Aikath Gyaltsen.[3] These writers have attempted to project a new sense of woman's identity that transforms her status from the victimized to the empowered by reconceptualizing the mother-daughter relationship. The shift from a poetics of suffering towards a poetics of individualistic empowerment is a noticeable trend in recent Indian women's writings in English. I will argue that this phenomenon reflects a concern for gender specificity which forms the basic principle of the French feminist writings of Luce Irigaray and Helene Cixious.

Feminism in Indian women's writings in English is, to a considerable extent, a by product of the western feminist movement. However, we cannot negate the contributions made by the Indian freedom struggle, and the specific political, social and economic problems that interest the Indian writer. Hence, it would be important, before we proceed any further, to situate this feminist discourse within the framework of Indian English prose fiction. According to Aparna and Vinay Dharwadker[4] three different frames generate three distinct themes in postcolonial Indian English fiction. The first frame encompasses the works of Mulk Raj Anand, Raja Rao and R.K. Narayan whose writings offer what Bhabha would term discourses of the Nation. The second frame is antithetical to the first inasmuch as it offers an anti-national or transnational allegory as in Rushdie's fiction. The third creates what is known as an East-West dialectic. In this context, the Dharwadkers cite the works of Jhabvala, Anita Desai and Amitav Ghosh.[5] To the three frames observed by the Dharwadkers, I would like to add a fourth one that generates feminist discourse. These writings have contributed progressively to a definition of the feminine identity and aesthetics.

Undoubtedly, the interaction of gender identity and national identity is an important aspect of postcolonial women's writings. Postcolonial women writers are faced with a dual situation—rejecting essential national metaphors of feminine identity and simultaneously constructing a collective national identity for women.[6] In Indian English writing (also observed in regional literature), the crux of feminism is the Indian woman caught in the transition from tradition to modernity. The women in fiction reflect the writer's sense of bewilderment and vulnerability. On one hand, they are portrayed as symbols of growth and fertility and on the other, they appear as symbols of withdrawal and regression. Obviously, these works do not offer solutions, they represent the crisis arising from the women's situation.

It is common generalisation that much third world literature is caught in psychological realism (a central trait of the nineteenth century European novel) whereas first world literatures have graduated into language games. In "realist" novels, the aim is to represent the interaction of moral and psychic development of the central characters with their surrounding social world. It is for this reason that these narratives have to stay within the boundaries of the actual if they have to maintain the illusion of being true to life. In a sense most Indian women writers have been staying within the constraints of the realist norm. However, for those who wish to suggest alternative modes of existence and alternative destinies, it becomes a difficult norm to embrace. These writers have to explore other forms or explore linguistic experimentations. This is noticeable in recent Indian women's writings. Differing syntactic and narrative structures, deliberate mixture of colloquial and sophisticated language etc., contribute to producing texts that are far from realistic.[7]

In order to reconstruct their identity, women are beginning to write at the intersection of realism and experimentalism. Gradually breaking away from politically and the tradition of national allegories, more and more women novelists are portraying apolitical stories of individual selves that only incidentally belong to middle-class postcolonial India. As an English speaking 'westernized' Indian, I cannot help but ask myself if applying western oriented critical discourse to works of English educated westernized Indian women writing in English could make a relevant study? Feminism is a world-wide movement, whether literary, social or political, but it does have different constituencies. So, can an elitist liberal French feminism help a westernized Easterner know her own world? Or is it possible only for a native to analyze her own sense? Most definitely, deliberate applications of the doctrines of high French feminism to a different political and cultural situation could prove inconclusive. I am arguing that it is possible to apply some of these models to critique third world texts without falling into the trap of reductionism.

Attempts have been made by critics to arrive at a definition of a specific set of feminine aesthetics based on the female biology and experience. For example, themes like childbirth, breast feeding, menstruation, rape, sexual assault etc. But this invariably creates an aesthetics of suffering. The choice of the books that I have made for the purposes of this essay is dictated by the very fact that in these two books attempts have been made to move away from an aesthetics of suffering towards an aesthetics of joy. The shift reflects most certainly one of the principal aspects of French feminism which does not see women's liberation only as reproductive liberation and hence does not consider counter sexism as an end.[8] The dual vision of rejecting sexism and affirming feminism undoes sexism by recognizing that nature has programmed female sexual pleasure independently from the needs of reproduction. Such a vision naturally calls into question the traditional, patriarchal notions of femininity and motherhood and the mother-daughter bond.

Luce Irigaray is concerned with rethinking the mother-daughter relationship. She states that within the symbolic order, this relationship is deformed and motherhood has a limited meaning in a patriarchal discourse.[9] It possesses neither economic nor social status and at the same time, it is kept away from the notion of sexuality. Given the restricted meaning of mother, the separation of mother from daughter entails total loss since no other identity is allowed except maturing. The restoration of a mother-daughter bond even after the facts of gestation, birthing and suckling is important, because this displays a persistent effort against the sexism of millennia.

Much of Indian women's writings have focused on the man-woman relationship to describe, analyze and define the Indian woman's identity. The first generation of women writers recreated and retold the destiny of Indian women resigned to their condition in a patriarchal society.[10] Even though the more recent avant garde writers like Anita Desai, Gita Mehta, Shobha De, Uma Vasudev have stressed on the pleasures rather than sufferings of the woman's condition, much of their writing still retains the man-woman relationship as the pivot of narration. Their women succeed in carving an identity for themselves, defying societal expectations and emerging intact after a cathartic experience, but this self-representation is achieved with reference to the male. More recently, some writers have taken to celebrating the female-female bond, attempting to create new paradigms for the recreation of woman's identity. It is this trend that I will be exploring in my discussion here. The two books, *The Thousand Faces of Night* and *Daughters of the House*, challenge essential, generalizing definitions of motherhood by reconceptualizing the definition of the mother-daughter bond. In contrast to isolation and loneliness as the only response to the woman's condition in a patriarchal set-up, these writers seek other solutions that propose rejuvenation and joy in a set of different circumstances that subvert existing social patterns and values. They are able to achieve this, realizing their womanhood as being different from their motherhood. In *The Thousand Faces of Night*, it is the stifling presence of the Mother as a social figure in a patriarchal set-up that makes the protagonist question her Self. In *Daughters of the House*, it is the physical absence of the Mother that makes the narrator redefine herself as a woman. In the end both women subvert the prevalent dictates of the patriarchal systems and seek to empower themselves by giving a new meaning to the mother-daughter relationship. It is important to add here that in the Indian cultural context, reviewing this relationship is particularly symbolic when it concerns the relationship between a mother and a married daughter. Daughters are conventionally brought up to believe that their parent's home is a temporary abode and that it's the "husband's house" which has to be eventually considered as "home." Once married they are treated as honoured visitors when they "visit" their parents. But, "returning" married daughters cause shame to the family's reputation and are a source of despair to their mothers. In the light of this cultural background, the determination of the women in these two novels to review the meanings of "home" and "motherhood" takes on powerful overtones. "Above all, she felt a piercing ache to see her mother. But equally powerful was the nameless dead she only partly acknowledges: the dread of the familiar love, stifling and all pervasive." (7)

The Thousand Faces of Night is the story of Devi's quest for a self-image. Having failed to define her identity within the framework of the male orientated social structures, i.e., as a wife in an arranged marriage, or even as a rebellious lover, Devi finally returns to her mother, "to stay and fight and to make sense of it all," and to start from the very beginning. It is in relationship to her mother that Devi hopes to find an identity for herself. The text dexterously weaves in multiple narratives, of Devi, of her mother Sita, and of Mayamma. The many voices of the feminine "I" reconstruct effectively any unitary, male view of the woman. The story of Devi, a woman in the process of "becoming" on her own terms, is interlaced with the narratives of Sita personifying perfect motherhood and Mayamma whose motherhood is socially defined as failed.

As stated earlier, according to Irigaray, within the patriarchal culture not only is motherhood devoid of any social or economic value, it is also separated from the procreative instant, i.e., from the notion of sexuality. In short, awareness of being a woman is associated with motherhood and not with womanhood. In *The Thousand Faces of Night* this aspect is brought home to the reader through Mayamma's story. It is natural for a woman to be proud of her sexuality but society prevents her from feeling such pride. In Indian society, women having their menses are disallowed from temples and from participating in any religious ceremonies. Mayamma attains puberty as she is playing in the temple. In an ironic sense, her sexuality can be considered a divine gift, but to the priest the male bastion of religiosity and upholder of the patriarchal norms, Mayamma's gushing womanhood has tainted the sacred premises. "I looked down at the blood on clear white flesh, my heart overflowing with something like pride." (115) Hardly has she been able to recognize and enjoy her femininity, when she is violently brought back to harsh male reality with a slap from the priest for defiling the purity of the temple. "A maid has to be wed before her womanhood develops," and so Mayamma is married off so that motherhood could be imposed on her. Even if the narrative treats her sexuality as a divine given, it is ironic that her motherhood is not a biological "given" and she has to go through years of penance and humiliation before she finally conceives.

In reality, societal constraints do not permit most women to express their womanness as being specifically different from their motherhood. So, women writers profit from the liberty that creative fiction offers to use imagery from nature as a literary strategy to externalized female sexuality. Githa Hariharan uses the metaphor of the wild gulmohar as a new model of female sexuality as opposed to the conventional model of the jacaranda. In contrast to the Jacaranda "made for wafting spinelessly in the arms of brutal winds," (86) the gulmohur "usurps the purple numbness with her incessant chatter. . . . The tongue of desire leaps from the deep, green streaked recesses of the petals, the wetness wildly spreading." However, in the narrative, this blossoming image of sexuality is abruptly snuffed out by the juxtaposition of Mahesh's view of his wife's womanhood ("Any news . . . his eyes quickly apprise my body, all bones and flat stomach." [86]) and immediately after with Sita's endorsement of the eternal idea that motherhood bestows deep contentment on a woman. Fiction thus swings between realism and experimentalism, as the writers find themselves trapped between social reality and the desire to narrate an alternative identity.

There is no necessary co-relation between the existence of a powerful feminine imagery in Hindu religious tradition and an elevated status of women. Hindu women have suffered at the hands of societal attitudes. Some trace this oppression to fear of their dual powers of benevolent fertility and malevolent aggression. The myth of Kali does suggest an image of strength, self-determination and wholeness. However, male elites have fostered an ideal of women's spirituality that conflicts with Kali as a model of fierce, independent action. Women growing up in India like Mayamma and Devi are exposed to the beatified image of Kali, the Compassionate Mother and not the Terrible Mother. It is obvious that this excessive sweetening provided by male intervention is to downplay the more powerful, independent and sexual side to the image.[11]

Mayamma's narrative reflects the exploitation and failure of motherhood insofar as it has failed to create sustained life (the life giver is seen as a life destroyer, since Mayamma is held responsible for the death of her good-for-nothing son). Victim of society and her family, ill-treated by her husband first, then by her spoilt son, Mayamma finally finds refuge in the house of a rich relative Parvatiamma. Frail and old, she now replays in her mind the myths that she could not play out in her real life. She recreates another genealogy of women, through her silent endorsement of the radical actions of Parvatiamma and Devi. In what seems to be an ironic attitude of passive resignation, she appears to be spending her last nights in mechanical service to the same benevolent Goddesses who have denied any kind of happiness to her all her life.[12] But as she turns each "desiccated, shrivelled bead" round and round, invoking for each bead the name of the mother goddess, what she actually sees in her mind are the aggressive forces of Kali.

Physically unable to change the course of destiny, but having found the power to transform the male constructed benevolent gods into forces that she can identify with, in her mind if not in reality, Mayamma bids her daughters "to seek the river, miles away, where the dim forest gives way to a clear, transparent flood of light." (126)

Since both society and religion endorse creativity as a masculine domain, motherhood takes the limited significance of care and nature. Irigaray says that because of this reduced meaning, women often run the risk of compensating it with over investment, in "self-denial," in non-being or in an over-possessive maternity. Sita is burgeoning with over-protective maternity. Githa Hariharan's narrative demonstrates that motherhood is not a natural construct but a patriarchal ideal that Sita has built unto perfection. Sita has over-invested by effacing her "Self" in denying herself her womanness (symbolized by her violent renunciation of her music), in order to be an ideal wife and ideal daughter-in-law. She saw her femininity as an "illusion" and so she "seized it firmly by its roots and pulled it out of her soul till the enticing stems of the seven-noted scale came apart, broken and disharmonious in a cluster of pathetic twangs." (105) By giving up her music she was giving up the "veena toting Saraswati, all femininity and ambiguity" to take on another goddess, "the most ferocious of all charges." Modelling herself on the 'Terrible Mother' image of Kali, she meticulously planned the lives of her husband, her daughter and herself with clinical efficiency. She led her husband from promotion to promotion as he moved up the corporate ladder. When Devi was born, she found a new "veena" to play on. Sita quelled the slightest "rebellion" in her that threatened to erupt in the form of books, daydreams, and gods and goddesses. She planned Devi's education, dispatched her to America where in the "wholesome rays of an antiseptic sun," she would learn to overcome her monsters. She packed her husband to Africa on a prestigious assignment. However, the strain proved too much for him and he died of a cardiac arrest. She erased his memories just as efficiently as his body was disposed, quickly and efficiently in a modern sanitised crematorium, before returning to India and devoting her talents and well-disciplined energy to work on Devi. "Sita believed most in the power of her own magic." (107) Wisely she allowed Devi, recalled from America, to indulge in a few tantrums before she arranged for her to be dispatched this time to a "permanent destination": wifehood.

While Sita's success story exemplifies the perfect male construction of motherhood, the narrative deconstructs this vision in two ways. Firstly, the matter-of-fact tone of the text completely undermines the "construction" compressing Sita's motherhood into a "simple unfragmented one-viewed organism" and effectively calling in question the social construct of motherhood. At the same time, the irony underlying Sita's choice of role model as the aggressive goddess Kali as opposed to a more benevolent form of the divinity weakens the credibility attached to male endorsed, conventional "maternal" qualities.

In fact, on a metaphorical level, the operation of the gardener metaphor that strings the narratives of the three different women together calls into question the very nature of nurture. "She pruned and repotted it sensibly, as she did her plants and she did it in the belief that it would take in the soil, even if it was the soiled ground of a life devoted to being the ideal woman." (107)

Punning, word play and the elimination of an unitary subjective I, are some of the characteristics of disruptive feminine writing according to Irigaray and Cixious. Here, the play on the word "soil" deconstructs effectively "the parameters that Sita had constructed or allowed to be constructed around her." (107)

By interweaving three narratives, *The Thousand Faces of Night* displays multiple referents for a single signifier "mother." This text provides a contrast to *Daughters of the House* where interestingly, the referent "mother" is non-existent, but the "signified" is associated with different signs before the ambiguity is cleared at the end of the narrative with a specific definition of the signifier "mother" for the referent, Chchanda. In *Daughters of the House* the narrator narrates the happenings in a "house of women." What appears as a vulnerable feminine kingdom becomes transformed into a legal matriarchy when the protagonist gains legal rights to her property and rejects wifehood to assume motherhood outside the male construct of marriage.

The untimely deaths and irresponsible disappearances of the male members of the household have constructed a "matriarchy of Panditji's house"—a universe of nuns, young and old where Chchanda and her sister living with a spinster aunt and a widowed relative had no reason to fear "tyrants with penises." She has grown up to consider men as "episodic characters. Rather useless and disgusting." (15) Madhulika, the aunt, has filled in as the surrogate mother to the orphaned girls giving them so much care and love that they forgot that she was "a human and a woman." Chchanda is also unaware of her own blossoming womanhood. The pleasure she derives in jumping naked into the bottom of the river to steal the fish trapped in her neighbour's fish trap is more from the joy of having successfully played a prank than from an awareness of her feminine sexuality. Her blissful uncomplicated world devoted to loving her aunt is shattered by the arrival of a male, Pratap Singh, her uncle by his "surprise" marriage to her aunt. Ironically, it is her jealous rage at the sight of Madhulika displaying her "delightful clumsiness" to her "darling" that eventually brings Chchanda to perceive her aunt as a "woman": "She was beauty herself. . . . And she paraded her abundance, the fragile innocence of her breasts, her neck, her eyelids, her colouring." (22)

Just as she feared, the arrival of a "male" completely thwarts the peace of a matriarchy artificially constructed by circumstances. This male is perceived differently by the three women. For Madhulika, marriage to Pratap is her escape from that "demanding world" of Paro and the burden of imposed "motherhood" towards a world of "happiness." Of course, to Madhulika, being a woman means "having a right to marriage" and having someone else, a male, handle the finances of the household, thus effectively endorsing the male construct of wifehood. To Paro, deciding to marry as "my aunt had done, so late in life, was a matter of sheer lust, justifying nothing" and Pratap was sin personified! To Chchanda, Pratap is the rival who has stolen her "aunt" from her. Till the arrival of a male in the household, Chchanda has created her identity in terms of her aunt's love, Paro's care, her sister's quiet affection and most importantly in terms of "each stone and leaf of Panditji's house." The intrusion of a male jeopardises the precarious relationships. Ironically, the aunt's marriage never takes off, since from the very first day, Madhulika falls sick. Physically incapacitated by her vague pains, uncontrollable spasms and persistent rash (it was to be later diagnosed as a form of tuberculosis of the skin) she is confined to her yellow bedroom and can never assume her wifehood nor openly enjoy her womanhood. Madhulika's sickness provokes a critical situation. Whilst her aunt's sickness keeps the enemy physically apart from her beloved relative, it does not keep him out of the house. "This is my house!

But I choked with spite when I remembered that he slept in the yellow room. . . . Something was chilling the cockles of my heart: the thought of never possessing Panditji's house." (56)

More than with any person, Chchanda identifies herself with the house that symbolizes security and stability in the life of a girl orphaned by the death of a mother and the disappearance of an irresponsible father. "I turned to ask the house something. It was an old trick of mine to give it a face, transforming the door into a mouth, the windows into eyes, the cracks into wrinkles, the time, the season, the way I felt even gave it the changing expression I had come to expect. The house was serious now, the trees around it lugubrious and stiff." (134)

Ironically, her aunt's confinement to her yellow room, makes a hostile Chchanda become sexually aware of the intruding Pratap. Thrown into Pratap's company when she accepts his offer to be his assistant in Ranchi and seduced by the possibility of financial independence, Chchanda eventually becomes a victim of Pratap's lust. She becomes the lover of the despised "maternal Uncle" and in a perverted twist of circumstances, a rival of her suffering, helpless aunt. Her discovery of her sexuality in such a shameful setting is accompanied by her feeling of alienation from her own house. By allowing Pratap to possess her, it is as if she has allowed him to take over her house. "I stagger upstairs, on strap of my slip torn. . . . This is a house where I once knew my way by instinct: a house that doesn't know me anymore." (96)

Ultimately, it is the solid and permanent presence of the house, symbolizing judge, companion and mother, that helps Chchanda achieve her self-realization. Love and nurture, the two functions of motherhood are split in the persons of Paro (the one who cares) and Madhulika (the one who loves). Chchanda is deprived of a conventional mother image. So, the house (a material relationship) symbolizes the stabilizing factor in her life. It signifies "maternal" refuge and most importantly, it gives her a social status when she becomes its rightful owner. Thus, the narrative deconstructs the social notion of 'motherhood' by associating different referents to the diverse signified related to the signifier "mother."

What kind of solutions do these texts propose for the feminine condition? Both the protagonists reject the idea of defining themselves within a male framework. Chchanda in *Daughters of the House* who gives herself to physical passion realizes very soon that this accidental discovery of her sexuality is insufficient to create an identity around her "love" for Pratap. Initially, even Devi in *The Thousand Faces of Night* thinks that she could define her self-image with reference to her lover, Gopal. But the futility of the attempt is represented by her inability to understand his music. "She knew the man now, not his music." Gopal constructs his woman just as he constructs his music and hence Devi cannot discover her true self in his company. "You see . . . why this raga is like a woman? It is a raga that celebrates strength. It is a passion that gives direction to all the superficial pretty little phrases. You arrange them like props, so that the real heroine can emerge." (131)

Gopal views women as being superficial since they require a man to provide them with a meaning. His construction of a woman is not any different from Mahesh for whom everything dissolves into nothingness except Devi's "stubborn unrelenting womb" (93): "You look so fragile, so feminine. . . . It's hard to believe that you do not want a child," he comments. Gopal's music means to him what the yearning for a descendant had meant to Mahesh, her husband. In the patriarchal system, the only identity that a woman possesses is that which defines her in relation to a male; she is either his wife or his child's mother.

Devi's covering of the mirror with her silk saree as she finally leaves a sleeping Gopal is symbolic of her rejection of herself as a reflection of Gopal. "She looked into the mirror, but it was as if she was still looking at herself. It threw back at her myriad reflections of herself." (138) The mirror effect of the symbolic order projects a self reflective image of masculine identity. Devi has come to a point where she no longer wishes to see things and people around her as reflections but as themselves. "She covered the mirror with the silk so that the room suddenly became darker and everything the beds, the table, the sleeping body of Gopal, were themselves again, no longer reflections." (138)

Her self-realization is linked to her desire to represent things in her way, to construct her own language and her own expression. In order to construct a positive feminine identity she has to look for a different order of meaning in the colourful garden of female imaginary. This is symbolically represented by her re-entry into her mother's garden that is now wild and overgrown, but lush in spite of its "sand choked roots."

Similarly, in the case of Sita, the garden metaphor symbolically describes her progress towards self-realization. For years Sita had meticulously constructed her garden, nursed her plants, trained her creepers and potted specimens just as she had trained and controlled her husband and daughter. The results appeared gratifying. All pervasive and something, she had not allowed her daughter to make any choices for herself. She had so efficiently pruned and potted her Devi that her betrayal (Devi's abandoning of her husband) is the ultimate blow to her efficient endorsement of the male construct of motherhood. But it is this incident that shows her the futility of her "selfless mission" and the artificiality of her own construction. In fact, her unstinting devotion to her family had not been a selfless mission. Having given up the measure of her own selfworth, i.e., her music, she had to adopt "worldly indices" and other measures, to ensure her survival. Now, the betrayal drives her to take on the merciless exercise of introspection. It forces her to dig up the language that she had given up, her music and to make time for "self-realizations." In the end as the strains of music draw the waiting mother and the returning daughter together, there is hope that in forging a mother-daughter bond, each will be also to give herself a specific definition of womanhood. The image of the "wild and overgrown garden" which displays too much "lushness" metaphorically suggests Sita's transition from a "constructed" mother to a Self whose womanhood is not "pruned and potted" by societal conditions.

Irigaray suggests that the mother must give the daughter more than food. She could give her the gift of a language in place of suffocation and silence.[13] Of course this requires a new mode of language. Here, in *The Thousand Faces of Night*, it is the gift of music that the mother eventually learns to give to her daughter that symbolizes this new language. In this way, both mother and daughter can be represented as self-referential subjects and not as exchangeable objects for men. Irigaray claims that what is required is another language outside the symbolic order, that constructs a maternal identity but that will also include sexuality. It is only such a mode of expression that can permit the forging of a bond between mother and daughter and at the same time assure each of them of a separate identity. In *The Thousand Faces of Night*, music symbolically provides the solution of an alternative language associating itself both with the feminine and the maternal. Devi comes back to her mother to the inviting notes of the veena. The language that Sita renounced as a symbolic gesture of her self denial is what she eventually adopts as she waits for her daughter to return to her.

In *The Thousand Faces of Night* the stories of alluring, self-sacrificing, and avenging goddesses of the Hindu pantheon serve as a backdrop to the triple narrative. Fed by her grandmother on stories of paradisiacal palaces, heroic women, self-sacrificing heroines and women turning into men, Devi realizes that she can relate neither to the aggressive model nor to the benevolent model of femininity. As she prepares to leave Mahesh for Gopal, she shakes off the ghost of her father and takes on Gopal in her first attempt to write her own version of womanhood, well aware of the risks involved. "I will soar high on the crest of Gopal's ragas, and what if I fall with a thud, alone, the morning after? I will walk on, seeking a goddess who is not yet made." (95) Eventually after having rejected existing myths and role models, Devi creates a different destiny for herself as she seeks to find a renewed meaning to her relationship with her mother.

As for Chchanda in *Daughters of the House*, she renews her links with her house and gives herself a new identity by appropriating for herself the very tools that empower the males and subjects the females to submission. Having betrayed her aunt, guilty of an almost incestuous love, and pregnant, Devi rejects the false security of "the name of the father, his family, his money" by refusing to marry Pratap. "It all means something" to Paro who represents male societal norms. But Chchanda finds a different ending to her story where there is no need for compromises and unnecessary justifications.

Instead of succumbing to societal pressures, Chchanda decides to take advantage of the social ostracization that will be imposed on her and Paro. Unable to rely on any model, ancestral or contemporary, she writes herself into a new story where the future is her daughter. In order to marry her, Pratap's argument would be "his daughter," but Chchanda is prepared to use the same argument to consolidate her stand and to keep herself free of him. "Already conquered by Panditji's house, how could he overcome it now, in the name of the daughter of the house who had become its future?" (197)

According to Irigaray, the beginnings of patriarchy as we know it today which represents man as the legal head of family, tribe or state, coincided with the weakening of the female-female bond and especially the dissolution of the mother-daughter relationship. This relationship was destroyed to establish an order linked to private property and to the transmission of possessions within a male genealogy. Such a system ensured that property and children belonged to the same genealogy.[14]

Chchanda on a personal level is rewriting her identity by rejecting wifehood (a social and artificial relationship) to adopt motherhood (as a natural construct). On another plane, she subverts the law of patriarchy by assuring for herself the ownership of the house and making her matriarchy legal to give her daughter the name of the mother. She lives her shame, rejects social security and empowers herself by appropriating the right to ensure that property and the progeny belong to the same genealogy, that of the female. "Here I am with a family, a property, and therefore an address." (199)

Pratap, she realizes, would have married her to have a say in disposing of the rundown house. She therefore doesn't reveal to him the existence of a will drawn up by his wife that stated that he was a part beneficiary of the house. By using subterfuge against subterfuge, her act of refusing marital security becomes neither an act of selfish sacrifice nor martyrdom but an act of determined self assertion. "As if a child once conceived cannot be borne without a father." (186)

In *Daughters of the House*, the narrative displays a sense of identity as split, of an alert, wry awareness of a self watching a self perform. The self retains a comic cynicism towards the construction of identity. The presence of a kind of parodic resilience prevents the narrative from sliding into a purely confessional and emotional discourse. "It would have been more appropriate to have thought about playing Ophelia among those long reeds that look so becoming in the hair of drowned girls." (186)

This aspect of the narrative seems to be in accordance with Julia Kristeva's notion of identity as performative and in process.[15] It is interesting to observe the use of cross-cultural metaphors (Ophelia, Penelope, Phedra, Lochinvar etc.) in the text. Even though they tend to undermine the cultural specificity of the narrative, they can also be seen as images that challenge dominant ideological codes by dialogizing meaning.

Each of these two books look at a renewed conceptualization of the mother-daughter bond from a different perspective. As Devi in *The Thousand Faces of Night* walks towards her mother to learn about her womanness, Chchanda looks at her daughter for her self-image. Both have in their way rejected the idea of being reflections of the male, but instead of sinking into a despairing isolation, they have resolved to rewrite another bond, the female-female one. The solutions are not absolute, but for both Devi and Chchanda, there is hope and a sense of rejuvenation as the past is erased and the present becomes an experience to build a future. Far from creating a poetics of victimization, these narratives create a poetics of empowerment.

Deconstructing the patriarchal logic at the centre of a meaning system is elating. These texts offer a solution to escape a restrictive defining system but in doing so they do run the risk of falling into the trap of individualism and ahistoricism. Women are looking increasingly at texts to find a positive identity in opposition to demeaning cultural images. The question is "What kind of writing should be considered progressive?" Are the concerns of an Indian woman submerged in urban poverty similar to those of upper middle class Indian women like Githa Hariharan or Indrani Gyaltsen? I am also uncomfortably aware of my own situation which is also privileged, both economically and professionally. My argument is that feminism is as much a cerebral phenomenon as it is a bread and butter issue. Just as there are many first world feminisms, Indian feminism is varied in nature and objective. We are living in a post-structural era, where plurality is reality and this study has attempted to examine a microscopic fraction of an extended but diverse female consciousness.

NOTES

1. It was Showalter who has been responsible for focusing on women's writings. She pioneered the idea of gynocriticism in opposition to the negative feminist critique of male authored texts. See Showalter, *The New Feminist Critics: Essays on Women, Literature and Theory* (Virago, 1986). See also Veena Noble Das, "Feminism and Literature," *The Commonwealth Review*, IV, 1994-95. Quoting Cher Register ("American Feminist Literary Criticism: A Bibliographical Introduction" in *Feminist Literary Criticism*, ed. J. Donavan, University Press of Kentucky, 1989), she argues that feminism should be a tool for social improvement.
2. Githa Hariharan, *The Thousand Faces of Night* (New Delhi: Viking, 1992).
3. Indrani Aikath Gyaltsen, *Daughters of the House* (New York: Ballantine, 1991).
4. Aparna and Vinay Dharwadker, "Language, Identity and Nation in Post-colonial Indian English Literature," *English Postcoloniality*, ed. Radhika Mohanram and Gita Rajan (Connecticut: Greenwood Press, 1996).
5. More recently, as Dharwadker observes in this article, Indian fiction writers are displaying cosmopolitanism in treating postcolonial India. The previous generation of fiction writers sought to Indianize themselves or to develop an anticolonial position but increasingly this stand is giving way to a disregard for themes like colonialism and postcolonialism. A more cosmopolitan approach that accepts a new world order in a neo-colonial global economy seems to be the latest trend.
6. For a study of the image of women in Indian English fiction see Shantha Krishnaswamy, *The Woman in Indian English Fiction (1950-1980)* (New Delhi: Asian Publishing House, 1984).
7. See Gayatri Spivak, *In Other Worlds* (New York: Methuen, 1987), p. 267. Spivak observes that in some regional literatures, though outwardly realistic or in a reductive manner of speaking "true to life" the nature of the syntax and the structural conduct of the narration contribute to producing a picture which is far from realistic.
8. See Elizabeth Grosz, Sexual Subversions—*Three French Feminists* (Sydney: Allen & Unwin), p. 113 (Chapter on "Luce Irigaray and the sexual difference").
9. See Chapter on "Writing as a Woman: Cixious and Irigaray" in Pam Morris, *Literature and Feminism* (Oxford: Blackwell, 1993). According to Freud, the Oedipal crisis exiles the girls and renders them

unknowable to themselves. So, what is needed is a new language that will represent maternal identity and at the same time maintain the unity of the maternal bond. Irigaray does not aim to create a new language but to use existing languages to subvert the functioning of dominant representations that put forth singular claims to truth. Irigaray is concerned with reviewing the prevailing images of mother and daughter and the construction of other positive models. Both Cixious and Irigaray support a writing practice that defies a repressive symbolic order. Irigaray stresses on "multiplicity, fluidity and the erotic intimacy of touching" as constituting the female imaginary. To the male model of language as a mirror of masculine presence, she compares the feminine form of representation to the speculum. The surface of a speculum is curved and hence deforms the reflections of a male discourse. The curved shape corresponds with the physical specificity of the female body and hence this mode of self representation is founded on the intimacy of touch. Irigaray's aim to specify sexuality could lead to the problem of sexuality becoming the equivalent of subjectivity. Critics claim that the theories of both Cixious and Irigaray transform the political into the individual by placing an ahistorical importance on sexuality as excess. They also feel that their identification of it with an universal feminine subjectivity is potentially dangerous. However since Irigaray's form of sexual difference takes the form A/B and not A/A, i.e., a form of difference not based on ridiculing the subordinated term, her essentialism can be considered positive.

10. See Ameeta Mulla Wattal, "Feminism in Commonwealth Literature: A Difference of View," *The Commonwealth Review*, VI, 1995-96.
11. For a clear contact with the feminine dimension in Hindu religious experience, see John Hawley, Donna Wulff, ed., *Devi-Goddesses of India* (Berkeley: University of California Press, 1996).
12. See Tracy Pintchmann, *The Rise of the Goddess in the Hindu Tradition* (New York: State University of New York Press, 1994). According to the author, in the puranic accounts of creation, the Goddess brings about the creation of the manifest world through her transition from pure power to material matrix, from which ordered forms arise. She notes that beneficent goddesses are generally married and are sexually controlled by their husbands. She quotes other critics who state that it is primarily the motherly qualities of a goddess that determine her beneficence.
13. See Grosz, p. 124.
14. See Irigaray, *Le Temps de la différence* (Paris: Librairie Generale Francaise), p. 30. See Morris, pp. 136-51.

The Future Memory and the Metaphysics of Technological Space: Text in Flux as Narrative Strategy in Arundhati Roy's *The God of Small Things*

KANNAMMAL SRINIVISAN

Empires have packed up and gone. However one item that resisted being packed was the English language. It has remained with us long after the colonizers have left and goaded us to decolonize and write back to the empire. The Indian writing in English as a body of literature had shown to the world some of our great minds in the last hundred years. At the turn of this century as we are celebrating Golden Jubilee year of our independence, one of our writers has won the coveted Booker Prize (1997) for fiction. Arundhati Roy has taken the literary world by surprise. Not everyone positively reacts to her work *The God of Small Things*.

The reviews, responses and reactions have been varied from praises to downright condemnation. This perplexes one but Roy's work itself is as complex and perplexing as her reviews had been. Especially her narrative technique is very subtle and hitech that appropriates the mechanics of modern technology vis-a-vis the computer. The insert text facilities available in the computers could make any item transposed at ease and to view the effect on screen, Roy had freely transposed, edited-in and edited-out texts and her fiction vibrates with life. This is the very quality that distinguishes her fiction from being a mere document or the history of Southern India as the Booker Prize citation says: "With extraordinary linguistic inventiveness, Roy funnels the history of South India through the eyes of seven-year old twins."

While transposing the texts, the future time sequence is brought earlier and the past takes a place later than the future like in Roy's text: "SORROW, HOWEVER, was still *two weeks away* on that blue cross-stich afternoon, as Margaret Kochamma lay jet-lagged and still asleep." (266, emphasis mine) The transposed texts make future memory possible.

Jacques Derrida speaks of "a memory in advance" that offers "a rearview vision of a future."[1] The composition of fiction itself is indulgence in future memory for it gives accurate descriptions of events that have not happened. The insertion of texts makes future memory a possibility within the fictitious narrative itself. It could treat the presence as absence and absence as presence and thereby increase their relative values. This process endows exceptional quality to the elements thus treated like dead man returned to life. I would call this as metaphysics of technological space.

It is a fascinating experience to focus on the text's play with space and time. Roy's fiction jumps, runs and plays like a child—now running a few spaces with speed as if time is all important, then stops hourlong to inspect an unimportant object putting on innocence and all the time tricking people and escaping the control of authority.

The text opens describing Ayemenem in the month of May and slides to early June referring to the monsoon rains in Kerala, the time that Rahel comes to Ayemenem from America. In a few paragraphs from hence the text moves back in time, some twenty three years, to the childhood days of Rahel and Estha. Then it moves forward in few years, to speak of Ammu's (Rahel's and Estha's mother's) death. A few lines from hence it moves backwards further to the time of the birth of Rahel and Estha, the twins to Ammu in Shillong:

> Gentle half-moons have gathered under their eyes and they are as old as Ammu was when she died.
>
> Thirty one.
> Not old.
> Not young.

But a viable die-able age.

They were nearly born on a bus, Estha and Rahel. (3)

The text again moves fast forward to refer to the death of Sophie Mol, Rahel's cousin from London who had come to visit the Ayemenem House. The text refers to Velutha's imprisonment and also Estha's sojourn with his father at Calcutta as an immediate consequence of Sophie Mol's death. Suddenly the text jumps twenty-three years forward from the time of Sophie Mol's death to speak of Estha's return to Ayemenem house with his father rejecting him once for all and sending a letter of regret for not being able to accept him as one of the family: "And now, twenty-three years later, their father had re-Returned Estha." (9) With Estha's return to Ayemenem the text seems to settle down to examine the condition of Estha at present, who had stopped communicating with anybody: "Estha occupied very little space in the world." (11) As the reader seems to have some control over the text's movement, the text believing the reader's expectation goes back twenty-three years from hence to speak in detail of Estha's schooling, his interests, habits and adjustments when he had been with his father in Calcutta. The text again moves forward to the condition of Estha at the time of Rahel's return from America after twenty-three years, when she meets him at Ayemenem House. The text again moves backwards a few years before Rahel's return to speak in paraphrasing tones of the circumstances of the inmates of Ayemenem House that Chacko (Rahel's uncle) has emigrated to Canada, Mammachi (Rahel's grandmother) is dead, Baby Kochamma, Rahel's great aunt and Kochu Maria, the servant are the only occupants of the house at the time of Rahel's return from America. The text all of a sudden moves back and starts to speak at length of Rahel's schooling after her mother Ammu's death. Rahel is blacklisted and expelled from school. Later completing school, she joins school of architecture at Delhi and completes her degree. Rahel marries Larry and divorces him. As the story of Rahel goes on, the text suddenly puts a fullstop to it by saying: "Nothing mattered much. . . . So small God laughed a hollow laugh, and skipped away cheerfully. Like a rich boy in shorts." (19) The text hurries to talk of Rahel's work at New York after her broken marriage and her return to Ayemenem. The text in all importance, alludes to the age of Baby Kochamma's (Rahel's aunt) as eighty three at the time of Rahel's return to Ayemenem. Suddenly the text with all the leisure in the world moves backwards some 65 years and speaks at length of Baby Kochamma's school days, her crush for Father Mulligan, her leaving for America to study ornamental gardening and her return to Ayemenem to practise what she has learnt. The text alludes to Rahel's thinking about Kochamma's way of life: "*She's living her life backwards*, Rahel thought." (22) The reader wonders whether it is Kochamma who is doing it or it is the text that indulges in doing so.

As if it has ended the story, the text starts speaking of the point at which the story begins. Believing the text's opening description of Rahel's return from America the reader seems complacent enough that the story is about Rahel or Estha or about the inmates of the house of Ayemenem. Again, the text runs away from the control of the reader. These pickles and preserves of memory being examined, the text wonders about the time that all these things had begun. The text settles on the issue of fixing the time to Sophie Mol's coming home but slides to a time before the Marxists came, the British took Malabar, or the Dutch Ascendency, Vasco da Gama arrived, Zamon's Conquest of Calicut, Syrian Bishops murdered by Portuguese, Christianity arrived in a boat and seeped into Kerala or actually it began thousands of years ago or: "That it really began in the days when the Love Laws were made. The laws that lay down who should be loved, and how. And how much." (33)

So then the text moving back and forth infinite, smashes the boundaries of past and present and enters freely into future and back from there. This process nullifies time and invests the text a God-like power to look both ways, to the future which is at the same time the past and the past which is also the present and the future. It problematizes chronology and history. The reality that the text speaks is not the reality of history but the reality of human sensitivity, perception and emotion. The truth that the text seeks is a different kind of a truth, perhaps the truth of the depths of human passion, the deceptions, happiness, disappointments, shocks, joys, betrayals, love, fulfilment and everything that the human heart is capable of at varying degrees. The story of the human heart never centres on time but timeless and endless and knows no past or present or future. It is like those great stories that the Kathakali artist presents that we have always known but want to know:

> The Great stories are the ones you have heard and want to hear again. The one you can enter anywhere and inhabit comfortably. They don't deceive you with thrills and trick endings. They don't surprise you with unforeseen . . . you know how they end, yet you listen as though you don't. In the way that although you know that one day you will die, you live as though you won't. (229)

The process of telling the story itself is an exercise in wisdom, as the text bears the title "Wisdom Exercise Note Books" where Estha indulges in story writing. Though corrections sometimes are not carried out, the very exercise leads to depths of emotional experiences and awakens sense perceptions. The future memory offers the wisdom to understand the values.

The first section from pages 1-33 encompasses the entire story of the book. The rest of the book comprising of some 250 pages reworks on several of the issues mentioned in the first section to produce, in my perception, the multi-dimensionality of sense perception. The reworking is achieved through the intertexts, compounded texts and transposed texts. These several texts actually serve as the vertical, diagonal lines that enhance the depth, intensity and various light and shades of the same referent at different spatial and experiential levels.

This technique, I would say, is informed of the school of painting that uses the same objects presented with different effects at different times of the day to show the effect of light and environment over the object. It could efface the structure and dimensions of the object and the same object viewed with a different shade of light gains structure and dimensions. The death of Sophie Mol alluded to by the text with dead pan expression right in the first section is devoid of any emotion and pain: "The Government never paid for Sophie Mol's funeral because she wasn't killed on a Zebra crossing. She had hers in Ayemenem in the old church with the new paint." (4) It is colourless, dull and shocks the reader for the very same qualities. However the shock that the reader gets for different reasons although, nevertheless is the shock that the news of Sophie Mol's death created when it first floated down to the inmates of Ayemenem House. The stunning news brings the paleness to the face as the object is painted with a bright sunlight falling on, deconstructing its structure. So too the death of Ammu and the imprisonment of Velutha are cited.

Darker and thicker lines are used for the sketch of Sophie Mol's death when the text gives it the stress at the end of Section I: "Still to say that it all began when Sophie Mol came to Ayemenem is only one way of looking at it." (33) The other lines in the picture of sense perception, so as to say, are drawn in the second section, titled "Pappachi's Moth." (34-87) It opens with the entire family travelling to Cochin to receive Sophie Mol and her mother arriving from London. The text stops just with the mention of Sophie Mol and slides to other texts. Several accounts that these texts recount and intersect the reference to Sophie Mol's arrival which is deferred till the 8th section of the text, serve to shade up the intensity and depth of the incidence of Sophie Mol. Pappachi, the grandfather of Rahel, was an entomologist. He suffers betrayal in his academic pursuits. Mammachi's (grandmother of Rahel) tortured life and Baby Kochamma's unrequited love for Father Mulligan, Ammu's loveless childhood bring up the tragic background. Yet at the same time these lines draw a picture of intense emotions and suffering on their own as Ammu's character gains tragic proportions. At one angle Ammu's life shades up the tragedy of Sophie Mol and Rahel and Estha and in another angle tragic lives of these children enhance the tragedy of Ammu.

The transposed texts compounded of passions of various characters like Pappachi, Mammachi, Ammu, Margaret, Baby Kochamma, Chacko, Sophie Mol, Rahel, Estha and Velutha, instead of being merely embedded texts, criss-cross each other and deepen the depths of emotion and intensity of passion. Every section of the text has the intertexts that in various angles and at various length stretch up and contract to give the tint. These texts at different stages are engaged in different process of drawing—it sketches, fills up the details, draws the background, thickens the lines, stretches, shrivels, shades up, brings in colour and the text sometimes moves back to see the effect.

Sections three and four speak of Estha and Rahel and give details of Velutha's revolutionary character. The happy childhood of Estha with its own shocks contrasts his grown up condition of complete isolation. They help to perfect the pictures of the strong passions of Velutha, broken dreams of Rahel and Estha and Ammu's tragic end that is closely connected with these three people. Comrade Pillai's subversive activities are alluded to as a connecting line to Velutha's tragedy. An intertext in section five titled "God's Own Country" endows the river, where tragedy of Sophie Mol took place, with supernatural powers. The ghastly skull smile of the river gains a ghostly dimension. The painted plastic watch of Rahel, which she had owned as a child and lost it on the day of the tragedy of Sophie Mol, is found again after twenty-three years, with the time painted on it;

> Something lay buried in the ground. Under grass. Under twenty-three years of June rain.
> A small forgotten thing.
> Nothing that the world would miss.
> A child's plastic wristwatch with the time painted on it.
> Ten to two it said. (127)

The time of Sophie Mol's tragedy is frozen. This effect of an emphasized, darkened spec is achieved through the transposed text's future memory.

In section six entitled "Cochin Kangaroos," lighter shades are applied with a parody on Baby Kochamma's quoting Shakespeare and Rahel and Estha playing the part of Ambassadors of India. The next section shades the events with darker colours with the sinister comment: "Things can change in a day." The text mentions Ammu's death with objectivity: "Ammu died in a grimy room in the Bharat Lodge in Alleppey, where she had gone for a job interview as someone's secretary. She died alone. With a noisy ceiling fan for company." (161) Her funeral also is described as routine: "There were no tears." (163) Nevertheless, the text is suffused with the sense of loss of Rahel, perhaps felt later and thus succeeds in painting the death of Ammu in double shade:

> The heat lunged out at them like a famished beast. Then Rahel's Ammu was fed into it. Her hair, her skin, her smile. Her voice. The way she used Kipling to love her children before putting them to bed. . . . Her good night kiss. . . . She was their Ammu *and* their Baba and she had loved them Double. (163)

Section eight entitled "Welcome Home Sophie Mol" speaks of the responses of the people at Ayemenem house to Sophie Mol's arrival from London, interspersed with a transposed text of Chacko's "Men's Needs" or his libertine relationships gaining sanctions in Ayemenem House. This puts into relief the injustice meted out to Ammu, based on her gender and Velutha based on his caste, for their relationship. The text then turns to lighter shades of recounting Sophie Mol's arrival. The intertext of Ammu's loveless, unhappy childhood is contrasted with that of Sophie Mol with the comment: "As she grew older, Ammu learned to live with this cold, calculating cruelty." (181) Discontinuing further elaboration, the text brings in Velutha's love and friendship for the children.

The next section elaborates on the drama enacted by the three children Rahel, Estha and Sophie Mol and the joy and happiness they find in each other's company. The text commenting on Velutha and Ammu's death in a transposed intertext slips to great emotional depths:

> He left behind a hole in the Universe, through which darkness poured like liquid tar. Through which their mother followed without even turning to wave goodbye. She left them behind, spinning in the dark, with no moorings, in a place with no foundation. (191-92)

As of now a clear picture emerges with the tragic shades filled in that Sophie Mol, the sophisticated loving, innocent, lonely child finding relationship, friendship and identity is to be struck to death in the swirling waters which she believed. Section ten entitled

"River in the Boat" instead of speaking of the death of Sophie Mol indulges in thickening the lines of the picture and shading the background to the tragedy in speaking of the preparation of the children to take a boat across the river. The text again defers the ultimate tragedy with the recipe on Banana Jam. Sketches on Vellya Paapu, Velutha's father who is to play the crucial role of exposing Velutha's rendezvous, appear with the omniscient comment that History had chosen him to set the Terror rolling on to Velutha. The text takes care to heighten the friendship of Velutha with the children so as to deepen their tragic perception in his loss. Mystery is mixed with the tragic colours with references to History House where the children plan to go and the presence of ghosts and ominous thoughts of caution enter the consciousness of children: Thought one is that anything can happen to anybody; thought two is: it's best to be prepared; thought three: a boat.

The next section entitled "The God of Small Things" emphasizes on future memory of those terrible things that are to happen: "But that would be Later. Lay Ter." (225) The detailed account of the passions of Velutha and Ammu with its dream-like quality are given. Those future happenings in the room of Ammu that the text compounds, colour the presence of Ammu and put her existence for Rahel in relief. The bedroom in which Ammu stood now is the same room that she would lock herself, be locked by Chacko, whose door that Chacko would batter down and order Ammu to leave the house, the same room where Ammu lovingly hemmed the ends of Rahel's ribbons, in which Estha packed and left for Calcutta, the room to which twenty-three years later Rahel would return.

In the next section the text takes elaborate detour in speaking of Kathakali performances where Great Stories are said for the wisdom they offer and not for the thrill endings. But the detour actually turns out to be the epic proportions of the tragedy; the tragedy that is spun from the human heart; the tragedy of the "hidden fish of shame in a sea of glory." (230) The tragedy is deferred but the background is thickened and shaded before filling in the main picture. The next section entitled "Pessimist and Optimist" goes back to the day of Sophie Mol's arrival at Ayemenem, then talks in detail of her parents' courtship, their separation, Sophie Mol's birth and the remarriage of Margaret, Sophie Mol's mother and the death of her second husband. The picture of Sophie Mol's tragedy emerges in fullness when the news of her death reaches: "In the morning when Mammachi and Baby Kochamma got news of a white child's body found floating downriver where the Meenachal broadens as it approaches the backwaters. (252) The text uses flat tones here. Later, it captures the depth and intensity of Margaret's pain at her only daughter's death:

> When Margaret Kochamma saw her little daughter's body, shock swelled in her like phantom applause in an empty auditorium. It overflowed in a wave of vomit and left her mute and empty-eyed. . . . She had come to Ayemenem to heal her wounded world, and had lost all of it instead. She shattered like glass. Her memory of the days that followed was fuzzy. Long, dim hours of thick, furry-tongued serenity (medically administered by Dr. Verghese), lacerated by sharp, steely slashes of hysteria, as keen and cutting as the edge of a new razor blade. (263)

The next section speaks of the parts played by other characters in Sophie Mol's funeral. Curiously enough, Rahel has illusions of Sophie Mol getting up from her grave and joining Estha and herself. This becomes real to Rahel. The pain had come to live with them, though "Sophie Mol became a Memory, while The Loss of Sophie Mol grew robust and alive. Like a fruit in season. Every season." (267)

In the next section the tragic figure of Velutha gets final touches with a detailed account of Comrade Pillai and his Judas-like betrayal. The final touches to this picture are given in the ensuing chapters, that speak of the tragic circumstances that lead to Sophie's death, the children leaving Ayemenem House, and the whole lot of changes taking place. This is always referred to by the text as that one day, the day of Sophie Mol's death that could change the lives of so many people. The day also happened to be the day that the 'cost of living' was high for Ammu and Velutha and they paid a heavy price. The ensuing sections draw the edges and give final touches to the picture by additional and minute details of Sophie Mol's death and Velutha and Ammu's tragedy. The text ends (!!!) with a "Tomorrow." Perhaps it signals that there is no end for the emotions and passions of the human heart where the dead are not really dead. Those situations charged with human emotions would be worked and reworked for possible corrections and better perceptions.

The transposed texts, the future memory and the intertexts problematize the linear time sequential narrative. The text influx serves to bring the intensity of emotions felt and depths of passion experienced. The experiential space simultaneously deepens and expands. The spatiality of experiential plane is not based on time but on the human energy to feel deeply, and experience intensely the dimensions of human relationship. The back and forth movement of the text in time nullifies time sequence and history. Therefore the truth the text is after is not the truth of history but a higher and at the same time a deeper truth of the hearts that throb in intense human relationship. Arundhati Roy revolutionizes the writing technique and transfers it from the physical plane to the software technology.

NOTES

1. Jacques Derrida, "Racism's Last Word" in *Race, Writing and Difference*, ed. Henry Louis Gates (Chicago: Chicago University Press, 1986), p. 330.
2. Arundhati Roy, *The God of Small Things* (New Delhi: IndiaInk, 1997).

Manju Kapur's *Difficult Daughters*: An Absorbing Tale of Fact and Fiction

SUMAN BALA and SUBHASH CHANDRA

The year 1998 registered a remarkable growth of novels in English. Notable amongst these are Mulk Raj Anand's *Nine Moods of Bharata*, Shiv K. Kumar's *A River with Three Banks*, I. Allan Sealy's *The Everest Hotel*, Amit Chaudhuri's *Freedom Song*, Sudhir Kakar's *The Ascetic of Desire* and Manju Kapur's *Difficult Daughters*.

It is interesting to note that the credit for popularizing Indian fiction goes to the various awards that the writers have received in the recent years viz. Booker Award, Commonwealth Writers Prize and the recently-introduced Crossword Book Award. Among these, Crossword's is the only prize that is confined solely to Indians.

In India, shopping for books has always been thought of as a book-lover's hobby. Existing bookstores, with their dreary, dusty and browser-unfriendly atmosphere, have discouraged all but the serious book-buyers. Crossword has been able to change this by designing large, spacious, well-laid out stores, with bright cheerful interiors that encourage people to stay and browse. Simple innovations such as methodical classifications, clear signages, a dedicated enquiry desk, electronic POS and inventory control systems and attractive displays make looking for books a much more pleasurable experience. A welcoming cafe and toilets within the store help to ensure that customers are able to spend several hours without having to leave.

With book stores in Bombay, Delhi, Ahmedabad, Pune and Nashik, Crossword is India's fastest growing chain. It is committed to promoting good reading through book promotions, literary events and discussions. The Crossword Book Award is yet another attempt at putting the focus back to reading and rewarding the best of Indian writing and good publishing. The judges for the award in its first year ever were the poet Adil Jussawala, the novelists Kiran Nagarkar and Mukul Kesavan, and academics Malashri Lal and Meennakshi Mukherjee. The cash prize of two lakh rupees for the year 1998 went to I. Allan Sealy's *The Everest Hotel* for its evocative prose, clear-eyed contemplation of death and love with humour and precision. The runners-up were *Difficult Daughters* by Manju Kapur, *The Madwoman of Jogare* by Sohaila Abdulali, *Across the Lakes* by Amal Chatterjee and *Tivolem* by Victor Rangel-Riberio.

II

Difficult Daughters is perhaps the most readable of the Indian novels published in 1998. It is therefore worth discussing the writer and the novel. Manju Kapur, born in Amritsar, is a senior academic. She teaches English at Miranda House, University of Delhi, and has four children. It took her five years to do research at Nehru Memorial Museum and Library at Teen Murti House for writing her debut novel *Difficult Daughters*. It involved a lot of hard work. As Manju Kapur says, "I had to rewrite the book eight times over seven years. And each time I thought I had finished the book." When Manju Kapur did not find any Indian publisher forthcoming to bring out her novel, she approached Faber and Faber in England. They published it after the suggested changes were made. Later it was published by Penguin India and was nominated for the Crossword Book Award, widely regarded as the Indian Booker Prize.

Difficult Daughters has been well-received by one and all. Urvashi Butalia of Kali for Women was struck by the simplicity of Manju Kapur's writing style: "There is no gimmickry in the language, as we see in some other books." The novelist Mukul Kesavan commends *Difficult Daughters* as "a first-rate realistic novel about a daughter's reconstruction of her troubled past, hinging on her mother's story." Actually it is a story of a daughter's journey back into her mother's past to reconstruct memories of her mother as the daughter she had been. The narrator visits the houses where her mother had breathed, meets her friends and acquaintances to retrace the dead mother's footsteps through time and space to tell a story that is unique and yet quite familiar.

Based on the factual events of India's partition, the story inextricably weaves the fictional tale of a Punjabi family covering three generations of women. There is Ida, the narrator, who has left behind her a disastrous marriage, and is a divorcee. There is Virmati who married for love an already married professor. And there is Kasturi, mother of eleven children, who comes to terms with a daughter who insists on studying and spurns marriage.

The novel has certain autobiographical touches. Like Virmati, Manju Kapur teaches in a college. She had a traditional upbringing and her mother's priority for her daughter was marriage. As Manju Kapur says, "Conflict between daughter and mother is inevitable, and I suppose I was a difficult daughter. The conflict carries on through generations because mothers want their daughters to be safe. We want them to make the right choices—'right' in the sense that they are socially acceptable. My mother wanted me to be happily married, I want my daughters to have good jobs." Her parents were well-placed Arya Samajis, like Virmati's relations. Her father, like Virmati's husband, was a professor before he became a bureaucrat. The jacket of the book carries the picture of her mother on the front cover and that of her father on the back.

III

The novel opens with a cryptic statement: "The one thing I had wanted was not to be like my mother."[1] These words are spoken by the young narrator, Ida. Every text contains several entry points. For this novel, the narrator's opening words constitute one and we would like to explore and analyze why she did not like to be like her mother, and then relate the answer to the larger issue of patriarchy, which denies woman voice, choice and freedom.

Set around the time of partition and written with absorbing intelligence and sympathy, *Difficult Daughters* is the story of a woman torn between family duty, the desire for education, and illicit love. The protagonist Virmati is the eldest child of the ever-pregnant Kasturi. She looks after ten younger siblings. However, she refuses to settle down to marriage and child-bearing after the high school qualification. She falls in love, instead, with the romantic Oxford-returned professor who lives next door and is already married. Caught in hopeless illicit love, she breaks her engagement with a suitable decent boy Inderjit, attempts suicide, and finally seeks refuge in further study. She goes to Lahore to live alone and study further. She goes to Nahan to work as a principal in a school. When she eventually returns to Amritsar as the professor's second wife, she has read more books and gained more varied experiences than girls of her time and society were expected to. However, her stay in the professor's house alongside his furious first wife creates irrevocable lines of pain around her.

Virmati's initial rebellion against her very traditional Arya Samaj family, consisting of her parents, her paternal grandfather, and Aunt (father's sister) in first postponing her marriage, and then refusing to marry the person she was engaged to, constitutes a radical rebellious act, which predicts an individual, who would go on to carve out a niche for herself, and make a personal exemplary, feminist statement. Her stoic and heroic suffering for the sake of her love, and marriage with professor Harish Chandra, who is already married to Ganga and has a child, point towards a "self" which is tenacious and assertive.

But her acceptance of the treatment meted out to her by her lover, the professor, totally belies these expectations. The professor's pursuit of Virmati even after she has been sent to Lahore as a part of punishment to study in women's college, his renewing sexual relations with her with full ardour, but his reluctance and constant postponing of the marriage in spite of her frequent entreaties to do so, are instances of the gratification of the male "desire." Male ego-centricism blinds men to the situation of women, who may be placed in agonizing circumstances on account of their relationship with men. Professor Harish Chandra seems to be enjoying the best of both the worlds: in Ganga his first wife, he has a servant who keeps his house tidy and his clothes washed, rears up his children and caters to his mundane needs and simultaneously he has Virmati, who fulfills his need for intellectual companionship which his docile and homely wife cannot offer.

Virmati's success in getting married to the professor, after her threats to sunder her relationship with him, however, does not get her any space in the family. The combined anger and resistance of Ganga and Harish's mother force Virmati to withdraw into her tight corner in the house, with Harish telling her that she has him and, therefore, should not bother about other things. It is interesting to note, however, that Virmati, who has acquired high education at a time when very few women were educated, longs to play the role of a traditional housewife. She wants to wash Harish's dirty clothes which she is not allowed to.

Also her education notwithstanding, it is always Harish who is represented as very knowledgeable, explaining and expounding ideas and ideologies and aesthetics. Ensconced on a higher intellectual pedestal, one senses, at times, a condescending strain in the tone and tenor of his explanations of events and issues to Virmati. Throughout the novel, the relationship between the two, even though a loving one, comes to us as an unequal one.

A notable example of the subdued and suppressed position of Virmati comes to us in the episode in which Virmati suggests the name Bharati, for their newly-born daughter. The name is dismissed as inappropriate by the professor, who does not deign to offer to be polite or persuasive. In his characteristic highhanded fashion, he is brusque and impatient. We would like to reproduce the short conversation:

> "Bharati," suggested Virmati as a name.
> "No," said Harish.
> "No? But why? I thought with the birth our country . . ." (225)

Virmati is cut short and is not allowed to offer her complete reasons, whereas Harish gives his detailed reasons. It is beside the point that the reasons given by him are also right but what is of significance is that Virmati is not even heard out fully. As Vandita Mishra points out in *The Pioneer* of 1 August 1998:

> Kapur never permits Virmati any assertion of power or freedom. Because even as she breaks free from old prisons, she is locked into newer ones. Her relationship with the professor, for instance. While it does provide an escape from a loveless

> arranged marriage, it is itself furtive and claustrophobic, offering only a stolen togetherness behind curtained windows. Even years of studying and working alone do not give her the confidence to strike independent roots and grow. She hovers uncertainly at the edge of each new world, never entering, lest the professor should call and not find her near. Eventually, marriage to the man of her choice is no triumph either. As second wife, she must fight social ostracism outside the house, and compete for the kitchen and conjugal bed with Ganga, the first wife, inside it.

The book ends, as it began, with the angry Ida's comment: "This book weaves a connection between my mother and me, each word a brick in a mansion I made with my head and my heart. Now live in it, Mama, and leave me be. Do not haunt me any more." (258-59)

It could, perhaps, be argued that the novel portrays India of the forties, a conservative period, comparatively, when women could not assert. But then the two factors which enable the modern woman to assert are education and economic independence—the latter more so. Therefore, Virmati comes to us as a modern woman, being both educated and having a job before marriage.

Virmati's positioning points to the larger issue of women's oppression and muffling which even education and the prospect of economic independence cannot end. The reasons for that is the cumulative brainwashing and social engineering done by patriarchy, which turns woman into a speculum, as Luce Irigaray puts it, of the male, with no distinctive features of her own. Hence, it could be argued that the whole novel is an answer to the narrator Ida's unambiguous declaration at the beginning that she would not want to be like her mother.

NOTE

1. Manju Kapur, *Difficult Daughters* (New Delhi: Penguin, 1998), p. 1.

Girish Karnad's *Tughlaq*: History in the Future Tense

NIBIR K. GHOSH

> Those who do not remember the past are condemned to repeat it.
>
> George Santayana

"God, what's this country coming to?" This exclamatory statement could very well be taken to be the lament of any ordinary Indian citizen in the contemporary context. But, amazingly, it is a statement uttered by an old man at the very outset of Girish Karnad's *Tughlaq*. The scene is the yard in front of the Chief Court of Justice in Delhi. The year 1327 A.D. Six centuries later, disillusionment still seems to be a factor which unifies the reign of Muhammad-bin-Tughlaq with that of postcolonial India caught in the vortex of an endless crisis.

Karnad's magnum opus *Tughlaq* (1964) is a veritable link between received history and its relevance in the contemporary frame of reference. "History," says E.H. Carr, "is a series of accepted judgements" but "facts and documents by themselves do not constitute history."[1] As a result, the play also offers useful insights into the inter-textual connection between history, historiography and the creative mind of the artist to reveal how a historical narrative related to the society of the past can serve as a key to the understanding of the present.

Girish Karnad's essential concern in the play revolves around Tughlaq who was not only "the most idealistic, the most intelligent king ever to come on the throne of Delhi, including the Mughals

. . . (but) one of the greatest failures also."[2] The story of the meteoric rise of a monarch endowed with visionary idealism and the subsequent decline and downfall of this tremendously capable man within a span of twenty years, provided Karnad with an excellent backdrop against which he could portray, project and foreground the discourse of visionary politics, the politics of demagoguery, the socio-cultural ethos governing fundamentalist ideologies and the crisis of a secular nationhood. Tughlaq, the man, seen against the historical attributes of the moment and the milieu in which he lived and reigned serves as a useful paradigm to enhance our perception not only of the pastness of the past but also of its presence. By juxtaposing the timeless as well as the temporal elements in the history of Tughlaq, Karnad has succeeded in displaying his acute historical sense which has enabled him to highlight not merely the present but the present moment of the past.

The play's abiding interest lies in the paradoxical personality of Tughlaq, the ruler. The elusive and haunting quality of the play comes from "the ambiguities of Tughlaq's character" related to "philosophical questions on the nature of man and the destiny of a whole kingdom which a dreamer like him controls."[3] Karnad's protagonist in the play is a faithful portrait and profile of the ruler as projected in *Tarikh-i-Firoz-Shahi* by Zia-ud-din Barani, who figures in the play as both historian and interpreter.

Karnad makes judicious use of Barani's account to recreate the paradoxical Tughlaq of history. Endowed with infinite powers of body and mind, Tughlaq stands out as the wisest and the most foolish muslim rulers of India. His extraordinary generosity, combined with his longing to kill the believers and the learned Sayyids, and at the same time to offer devotion to God, seems a very difficult trapeze balancing act. The play brings to the forefront the personality of Tughlaq with strikingly conflicting habits. He regards with contempt the names of his predecessors while professing a deep reference for the Caliphs. He does not hesitate to get rid of the evil doers by putting thousands to death on the slightest suspicion, but he remains deliberately blind to the mischief of rogues and murderers.

In the first scene of the play we find Muhammad Tughlaq expressing his delight and satisfaction over the manner in which justice works in his kingdom "without any consideration of might or weakness, religion or creed." (3) His dream is to perpetuate "greater justice, equality, progress and peace—not just peace but a more purposeful life." (3) Continuing in his vein of idealism he announces that to achieve this noble end he has decided to shift the capital of his empire from Delhi to Daulatabad. His rationale for such a decision is that "Daulatabad is a city of the Hindus and as the capital it will symbolize the bond between Muslims and Hindus which I wish to develop and strengthen in my kingdom." (4) It is evident from this statement that Tughlaq desires to build the foundations of his empire on the ideal democratic notions mingled with the catholicity of spirit which embraces diverse religions and cultures in a truly human attitude. By relocating his capital in a city of the Hindus, he hopes to develop and strengthen the bond between Muslims and Hindus in his kingdom.

Known the world over for his knowledge of philosophy and poetry, Karnad's protagonist, like his historical prototype, experiences a thrill in imagining the creation of a new world which he intends to rule not with the power of the sceptre in the style of a Muslim fundamentalist tyrant but by emulating the visionary idealism of the Greeks, Zarathustra, and the Buddha. Besides his decision to shift his capital to Daulatabad, the play shows how Tughlaq, tempted by the success of the paper currency in China, introduced the token copper currency in his kingdom, a scheme which ultimately failed.

Tughlaq's attempt to tread through the clear stream of reason by propagating communal harmony between Hindus and Muslims may be an excellent recipe for the symptomatic malaise of both fourteenth century and contemporary India, but such notions of harmony were then as are now, nothing but transcripts of utopian dreams. The seeds of disorder afflicting society on communal lines seem to have been sown centuries ago. Nurtured and nourished by mutual hatred and violence, these seeds of dissent ultimately led to the partition of the subcontinent and created almost similar conditions subsequent of the demolition of the Babri Masjid in recent times. The introduction of religion into politics to secure power over the masses in order to arouse their political consciousness has thus become a dominating factor in the game of power politics.

The concept of 'secularism' so enthusiastically espoused by Tughlaq as an accepted principle of governance has been bandied about in the last so many decades. It has been used and misused for political causes. Different parties of the same kind, based on religion, have often at one and the same time been described contrarily and opportunistically as secular and non-secular for political advantage. While advocating the secular cause, Tughlaq never seemed to have realised that his idealism would set him up against the Amirs, the Ulema, and the Sayyids who did not appreciate the ruler's lack of fundamentalism in approaching the holy *Koran*. It is not surprising therefore to see Tughlaq bewail:

> I can still feel the thrill with which I found a new world, a world I had not found in the Arabs or even the Koran. They tore me into shreds. And to be whole now I shall have to kill the part of men which sang to them. And my kingdom too is what I am—torn into pieces by visions whose validity I can't deny. You are asking me to make myself complete by killing the Greek in me and you propose to unify my people by denying the visions which led the Zarathustra or the Buddha. (21)

Tughlaq is warned by Imam-ud-din that the verbal distinctions that he sees between religion and politics are bound to rip him into two, a warning which seems to be valid in the context of contemporary Indian politics where 'secularism' seems to stand no chance of being cleansed of the cobwebs of self-interested meanings given to it. The contemporaneity of Karnad's play emerges from his identification of the variables and the constants which have controlled the power equation ironically in the world's largest democracy. It is not surprising, therefore, that religion and politics have become so intermingled that the destiny of the nation is being controlled by them. The propounders of Islam such as the characters like Sheikh Imam-ud-din and Sheikh Shihab-ud-din and even Barani deeply appreciate how Tughlaq has done a lot of good work—built schools, hospitals, made good use of the money (31) but they tell him that he must use all that God has given—"power, learning, intelligence, talent" to "repay his debt" by spreading "Islam round the world" (20) instead of trying to become 'another God.'

The fundamentalists take recourse to all the arsenals at their command to undermine the power and authority of Tughlaq. They accuse him of the crime of both parricide and fratricide and of the greater guilt of being generous and liberal to the Hindus. Akin to the noble Hamlet, Tughlaq can't help lamenting his fate of being surrounded by stratagems and intrigues: "I had wanted every act in my kingdom to become a prayer, every prayer to become a further step in knowledge, every step to lead us nearer to God. But our prayers too are ridden with disease, and must be exiled." (44)

The naivety of Tughlaq becomes apparent in his failure to realise how even in his reign religion is inextricably linked to politics. At the beginning of the play we find the Announcer informing the crowd of people how Vishnu Prasad, a brahmin of Shiknar, has won his suit against the Sultan himself and has received just compensation for the loss of his land which had been seized illegally by the officers of the State. In upholding the claim of Vishnu Prasad against his own authority, Tughlaq feels elated to see how he can dispense justice in his kingdom irrespective of considerations of might, religion or creed. Shortly after, we are informed that Vishnu Prasad is none else than Aziz, a low caste Muslim washerman who, masquerading as a poor Hindu Brahmin litigant, succeeds in exploiting Tughlaq's concept of justice and impartiality. Interestingly, Aziz confesses to his friend Aazam that he chose to masquerade as a poor Hindu Brahmin simply because "a Muslim plaintiff against a Muslim king" (8) would not synchronize with the Sultan's idea of impartial justice.

The above incident reveals interesting sidelights. In Tughlaq's India it was possible for ordinary mortals like Aziz to exploit the politics of communalism to gain a stretch of land and to manage a post in the civil service "to ensure him a regular and adequate income." (3) In contemporary India the likes of Aziz may exploit similar situations to reach the apex in the pyramid of power. With a little astuteness it has become possible to use religion or caste in controlling the nerve centres of power. It is little surprising that recent elections in India have been won or lost on purely communal or caste lines.

When Tughlaq, the visionary idealist, sees the hue of truth

come shadowing over his bright ideal planet, he gradually turns into a ruthless demagogue. As his dreams of ruling by the power of benevolence, justice and impartiality lie shattered, the philosopher king soon turns into a ruthless tyrant. Unable to sustain his ideology of goodness for long, Tughlaq slides into the morass of despotisms. He proudly celebrates his right to slaughter people, to be known by his beloved subjects as "Mad Muhammad" and as "Lord of Skins." He does not hesitate in asserting that "not words but the sword—that's all I have to keep my faith in my mission." (66) The ruler who began with the "hopes of building a new future of India" has learnt to solve "all problems in the flash of a dagger." (42) He wanted to shift his capital from Delhi to Daulatabad with motives both pious and strategic for the security of the nation. But when his adversaries hatch a plot to kill him at prayer time, he states without any pangs of conscience: "I want Delhi vacated immediately. Every living soul in Delhi will leave for Daulatabad, within a fortnight. I was too soft, I can see that now. They'll only understand the whip. Everyone must leave. . . . Nothing but an empty graveyard of Delhi will satisfy me now." (44)

Tughlaq wanted to command by the power of trust and understanding but the vitiated atmosphere of a court dominated by the communalization of politics makes him ask Barani sadly: "Are all those I trust condemned to go down in history as traitors? Tell me . . . will my reign be nothing more than a tortured scream which will stab the night and melt away in the silence?" (43) Living 'dangerously' in the style of a Nietzschean hero, Tughlaq considers every conceivable unscrupulous means to be justified in acquiring and sustaining power and authority. He is adept in the art of silencing dissent and opposition as any contemporary demagogue be it Hitler, Mussolini or even Indira Gandhi during the Emergency era. Through a series of events Karnad shows how power, once rooted, is not easily shaken. Once a demagogue fails in transforming power into authority, the waning consent of the governed compels the demagogue to assume the role of a cruel and relentless despot. Tughlaq takes continuous recourse to methods of coercion to legitimise the power that he wields.

Tughlaq emerges as a shrewd politician who has learnt the art of transforming every adverse situation to his advantage. He invites the charismatic religious leader Imam-ud-din to address a public meeting and gives him the freedom of denouncing the policies of Tughlaq in public. The act may appear to exemplify Tughlaq's courage and integrity in allowing freedom of expression to prevail in his kingdom. This facade of impartiality and supreme objectivity comes to the fore when we learn that his soldiers have been sent from door to door to prevent them from attending the said meeting. His plan to eliminate Imam-ud-din projects him as a brilliant intriguer. Being made aware of his close resemblance with Imam-ud-din, he uses the latter as his emissary for peace against the approaching army of Ain-ul-Mulk, the Governor of Awadh and one-time friend of the Sultan. Dressed as Tughlaq in his exact likeness, Imam-ud-din approaches Ain-ul-Mulk and before he begins to speak the charge is sounded. Countless arrows pierce him to make him look like a 'gory porcupine.'

Similarly, when Sheikh Shihab-ud-din hatches a plot to assassinate Tughlaq at prayer time, he foils the plot with the help of his Hindu guards and stabs the Sheikh with such ferocity that even his soldiers are horrified. Then, with utmost cool, he makes a public announcement that Shihab-ud-din died a martyr defending Tughlaq against the nobles who came to kill him at prayer time. He assures that the Sheikh would be given a grand funeral. Ratan Singh, who betrays the Sheikh and discloses the plan which he himself has persuaded the Sheikh to execute, refers to him as "an honest scoundrel" who "murders a man calmly and then actually enjoys the feeling of guilt." (28)

Tughlaq's folly lay in his failure to understand the political pulse of his time. Embittered by the troubles and disorders engineered and nursed by interested pressure groups, Tughlaq resorted to merciless killings. Lacking the prudence and moderation of an emperor like Akbar, Tughlaq found coercion to be a better device than appeasement. His appreciation of Hinduism and his free and unrestrained association with Hindu ascetics offended the fundamentalist religious order of Islam. As a result, every project that he planned failed and brought in its train a series of new troubles. His campaign for the discovery of truth and his anxiety to stop the evil at its source, and administer justice and equity brought him into conflict with a body of people whose fault was unpardonable in his eyes.

In spite of Tughlaq's best intentions, his schemes of introducing copper currency met with failure. Tughlaq failed to realise that the intrinsic value of the copper coins amounted to very little like the modern bank notes. Besides, the copper coins, in the absence of the state control of the mints, could be easily minted in private houses. Tughlaq says in this context: "Only one industry flourishes in my kingdom. Only one—and that's of making counterfeit copper coins. Every Hindu home has become a domestic mint; the traders are just waiting for me to close my eyes." (55) When Tughlaq found the scheme impracticable, he recalled all the copper tokens, exchanging each at its face value for silver coins. As a result, so many of these copper tokens were brought to the treasury that heaps of them rose up in Daulatabad like mountains, thus straining the economy considerably. Tughlaq's impulsiveness in introducing such ambitious projects and the lack of farsightedness in visualizing the consequences of his own actions were instrumental in his schemes coming to nought.

Tughlaq had abundant sympathy for the downtrodden and the weak but such generosity and compassion were suitably exploited by characters like Aziz. Aziz not only deceives Tughlaq in the garb of Vishnu Prasad but also towards the end of the play kills the holy man Ghiyas-ud-din Abbasid and appears before Tughlaq in the guise of the deceased. He has the audacity to tell the Sultan: "I admit I killed Ghiyas-ud-din and cheated you. Yet I am Your Majesty's true disciple. I ask you, Your Majesty, which other man in India has spent five years of his life fitting every act, deed and thought to Your Majesty's words?" (82) Though annoyed by the insolence of Aziz, Tughlaq does not punish him for his crimes. On the contrary, he allows Aziz to masquerade as His Holiness Ghiyas-ud-din Abbasid. He is even prepared to send him to Deccan as an officer of the State. The historian Barani warns him against committing such folly. He suggests that criminals like Aziz only deserved to be killed since he cannot see any logic in the Emperor's kindness for Aziz. Tughlaq's reply in the form of a long speech provides the justification for his action:

If justice was as simple as you think or logic as beautiful

> as I had hoped, life would have been so much clearer. I have been chasing these words now for five years and now I don't know if I am pursuing a mirage or fleeing a shadow. Anyway what do all these subtle distinctions matter in the blinding madness of the day? Sweep your logic away into a corner, Barani, all I need now is myself and my madness—madness to prance in a field eaten bare by the scarecrow violence. But I am not alone, Barani . . . I have a companion to share my madness now—the Omnipotent God. When you pass your final judgement on me, don't forget Him. (84-85)

Like Khalil Gibran's 'Madman,' Tughlaq seems to have found both freedom and safety in his madness—the freedom of loneliness and the safety from being understood. The glorious ideals that he had visualized in attempting to make his empire 'the envy of the world' remain at the end mere optical illusions. The blinding madness of the day characterized by events of political expediency has relegated all logic into a corner. The only refuge left for Tughlaq at the end is in the haven of his own loneliness. Dogged by the despair of his own failures and disillusioned by his tragic sense of idealism, Tughlaq sadly tells Barani: "There is only one place to go back to now. . . . I have to get back to Delhi with my people." (84)

Tughlaq's act of shifting his capital from Delhi to Daulatabad and back again to Delhi suggests the tragic attributes of his nemesis. Reminiscent of an ideal tragic hero whose fall is brought about by his tragic flaw as well as by extenuating historical circumstances, Tughlaq's tragedy lies in his failure to reconcile his idealism with the historical imperatives of the situation in which he finds himself. Tughlaq's return to Delhi thus becomes symbolic of his going back to his own actions and paying for them to find peace. Girish Karnad has acknowledged in an interview that "*Tughlaq* is actually a play of a king who comes face to face with himself and finds peace in madness."[4]

Girish Karnad admirably records the flux and turmoil of the reign of Tughlaq to present a paradigm for an interpretation of politics in terms of certain ever-present fundamentals. He moves from the limited confines of Tughlaq's times into our own immediate context to see a temporal world relative to eternity. Knowing that the seamless web of human politics is woven continuously from past to present and that it repeats its design from State to State, Karnad examines all the fundamental issues relevant to the present Indian society and polity against the perspective of space and time. Highlighting the permutations and combinations of political patterns, Karnad succeeds in showing how historical change itself is as constant a factor as the issues governing the change. He rightly shows that the bane of Indian society is that religion, since the time of the first Muslim invasion, has never been considered for the theology of the faith it adopts but as organized institutions. The cluster of religious institutions in perennial defence of their vested interests and privileges have constantly followed the path in which religion lends itself to the political stratification of humanity.

Ideals are rooted in reality, but always project beyond it. Tughlaq's failure to comprehend this simple truth led to the crumbling of his empire. All his altruism and benevolence, self-sacrifice, dedication to the public good and a solicitude for human welfare seemed to be irrelevant in the context of the disorder of the times. His is the tragedy of an able ruler who failed to grow into a statesman and a leader, even though gifted with such an unexpected opportunity by fate.

Tughlaq's tragic tale is symptomatic of the inherited complex problems of Indian society. Time and again it has been proved that mere idealism, unrelated to the understanding of the times, cannot by itself help in reaching visionary heights. It is not surprising to note that akin to Tughlaq many Indian leaders who were themselves great ideal models of honesty and integrity failed to sustain their own visions in politics. It is common knowledge that chief architects of India's tryst with destiny—Mahatma Gandhi, Jawahar Lal Nehru and others—despite their innate idealism and commitment to the progress of the nation have more or less been reduced to mere footnotes on the margins of contemporary Indian history. People with the immaculate image of honest and clean politicians have proved disastrous as leaders of the nation. The ever-increasing criminalization of politics in India of today is indicative of the failure of ideal role models to govern the country. The play also goes on to show how hard measures imperative to the progress of the nation can never find acceptance with either the players of the power game or with the common populace. Recent Indian history bears evidence to the fact that a popular government fell simply because it saw compulsory family planning as an inevitable measure to solve the nation's problems. Rampant corruption has made the ideals of honesty anachronistic. All idealisms are nothing but mirages in the arena of power politics. The untenability of idealistic and visionary politics makes the play perennially contemporary. In a society poised between secular and fundamentalist ideologies, the parameters of Tughlaq's world bear close resemblance to the discourse of the modern Indian political and cultural experience. The play, therefore, enables us to judge Muhammad-bin-Tughlaq from the standpoint of contemporary India, despite there being essential differences between the characteristic features of the fourteenth and the twentieth centuries.

In his introduction to the play, U.R. Anantha Murthy writes how the play is a "dramatized version of Tughlaq's tortured, divided self."(ix) In the external action of the play, Anantha Murthy sees the enactment of the inner drama of Tughlaq: "Both Tughlaq and his enemies initially appear to be idealists; yet, in the pursuit of the ideal, they perpetuate its opposite. The whole play is structured on these opposites: the ideal and the real; the divine aspiration and the deft intrigue. Tughlaq is what he is in spite of his self-knowledge and an intense desire for divine grace. . . . In the end, Tughlaq and his kingdom are one in their chaos and he knows it." (ix-x)

Anantha Murthy attributes the reason for *Tughlaq*'s appeal to the Indian audience to the fact that "it is a play of the sixties and reflects as no other play perhaps does the political mood of disillusionment which followed the Nehru era of idealism in the country." (vii-viii) He has referred to Karnad's own comment in this regard to substantiate his inference. To view the play as a striking parallel to the mood of political disillusionment of the sixties is to limit it to being a period piece of temporal value. In fact what Karnad has been able to do with the historical narrative of *Tughlaq* is of much wider significance. By coalescing the social, political, and intellectual history of the reign of Muhammad-bin-Tughlaq into the personality of the paradoxical historical figure, Karnad has been able to offer a brilliant paradigm for comprehending religious and philosophical systems, social and political institutions, and the role of cult figures in the contemporary Indian parlance. By analyzing the fateful events of Tughlaq's times in the context of contemporary India, Karnad presents a moving parable of political idealism gone awry whose relevance would continue in the country's timeless existence. The manner in which Karnad has amalgamated the political significance of Tughlaq's reign with his aesthetic and emotional response to the Emperor who felt that he alone had the correct answer, shows Karnad's ingenuity in presenting historical truth beyond the limits of an academic landscape.

Tughlaq is by no means a straight realistic play, for, despite close parallels with its historical antecedents, it cannot be deemed to be a photographic imitation of history. Since truth, life, or reality is an organic thing which the poetic imagination can represent or suggest, in essence, only through creative and imaginative transformation. *Tughlaq* remains unique in that it allows its author the responsibility of dealing with reality and interpreting experience. The work is essentially not fiction but an effort at history; everything the characters are represented as doing, they actually did. But by investing the character of Tughlaq with the tragic flaw of human material, Karnad has leant enduring appeal and charm to the otherwise tragic tale of disintegration. He has allowed his narrative to mediate between the substance of power politics and the values in which power politics is based. Karnad has rightly restrained himself from pronouncing any final verdict for it is not an artist's job to judge historical events. What he projects is a distillation of history, a particular image of a perpetual situation. The characters skip out of their fourteenth century skins to address a twentieth century audience in the language of contemporary political expediency, showing, thereby, how great art by virtue of symbolic illumination would always comprehend and answer problems which remain quintessentially relevant to all times.

NOTES

1. E.H. Carr, *What is History?* (Penguin Books, 1961), p. 19.
2. Girish Karnad, "Interviewed by Rajinder Paul," *Enactment*, 54, June 1971, p.3.
3. U.R. Anantha Murthy, "Introduction" to *Tughlaq* by Girish Karnad (Delhi: Oxford University Press, 1972), pp. viii-ix.
4. Girish Karnad, "Interviewed by Rajinder Paul," p. 3.

Caste and Religion in Girish Karnad's *Tale-Danda*

A.R. SHUKLA

Girish Karnad has attempted various themes concerning past history, past and present values, and religious beliefs and myths of India. In that way he is deeply concerned with India and the Indianness. Karnad, it seems, has taken up a job to re-interpret and, if necessary and if possible, to re-structure the traditional values of social and political systems concerning caste. He is also concerned with the subtle meaning of Religion. In "his first play *Yayati* (1991) he re-interprets an ancient Hindu myth on the theme of responsibility."[1] But in *Tughlaq* (1972), a historical play on the life of Sultan Muhammad-bin-Tughlaq of the fourteenth century India, he shows Tughlaq as a complex personality who is "at once a dreamer and a man of action, benevolent and cruel, devout and godless."[2] M.K. Naik notes that "Karnad himself has suggested that he found 'Tughlaq's history contemporary' in that the souring of his idealism had a close parallel in the mood of disenchantment of the sixties after the passing away of Nehru; and this is another reason why the play was a success on the Kannada stage." (262) Here Karnad draws correspondences from the past to the present, from history to the real life to meet his thematic needs. In *Tale-Danda* (1993) he re-examines the need and structure of the caste system of India that was once, in the past, hailed as an ideal one. Picking up historical-cum-political background for his plot, he moulds his theme of Tale-Danda to serve his present needs. He writes, "I wrote *Tale-Danda* (1993) in 1989 when the 'Mandir' and the 'Mandal' movements were beginning to show again how relevant the questions posed by these thinkers were for our age."[3] These thinkers are those who condemned idolatry and temple worship. Indeed, they reflected anything 'static' in favour of the principle of movement and progress in human enterprise. They believed in the equality of sexes and celebrated hard, dedicated work. They opposed the caste system, not just in theory but in practice. This last act brought down upon them the wrath of the orthodox. The movement ended in terror and bloodshed." It is through the *sharanas* that the author advocates his philosophy. Basavanna, the great *sharana* saint poet is the mouthpiece to announce the author's views. However, the author's views are expressed also through the King Bijjala who is very close, in thinking and nobility, to the dukes in Shakespeare's plays. He also shares his views with Kakkayya, a *sharana* and an untouchable saint aged about seventy.

Ancient saying in the form of commandments, shariyats or Vedic mantras need to be reassessed and reviewed with the change of time and growth in understanding. A fresh outlook is inevitable to analyse the literary and the cultural stores which the past masters have left for us. Prakriti, a Chandal girl in Tagore's *Chandalika* (1933), says, "A religion that insults is a false religion."[4] Basavanna in Karnad's *Tale-Danda* says, "Some say this entire edifice of caste and creed, this poison-house of varnashrama, will come tumbling down. Every person will see himself only as a human being. As a bhakta. As a *sharana*. That is inevitable. . . . You know the most terrible crimes have been justified in the name of sanatan religion." (39) Arun Shourie, in his introduction to *Indian Controversies* (1993), states, "in each tradition there is much that is valuable, but also much that is malignant." (viii) Hence there is need of a new religion, a religion which can treat all human beings as equal. *sharanas* believe in this. In the words of Kakkayya, "There is no caste among *sharanas*, neither brahmin, nor cobbler." (38)

The major theme of Karnad's *Tale-Danda* is that of deconstruction of caste and religion to arrive at its real, proper meaning and to restructure the same for the benefit of the society and the country. In scene after scene Karnad gives new doses and fresh outlook to the set beliefs and rooted religious faiths. The traditional caste-system claims that a king is supposed to be a Rajput or a Kshatriya. The author gives a stunning dialogue taking place between Bijjala, the king and Rambhavati, the queen.

Bijjala: What is my caste? Tell me.

Rambhavati: We are Kshatriyas.

Bijjala: Your family—the Hoysalas, you may be Kshatriyas. But I am a Kalachurya. A barber. His Majesty king Bijjala is a barber by caste. For ten generations my forefathers ravaged the land as robber barons. For another five they ruled as the trusted feudatories of the emperor himself. They married into every royal family in sight. Bribed generations of Brahmins with millions of cows. All this so they could have the caste of Kshatriyas branded on their foreheads. (14)

Here Karnad achieves two aims. He shows that the king of Kalyan is not a kshatriya but a barber. Further he shows him full of insight and noble thoughts, perhaps to show that deep insight, noble character and ideal administration are not the inborn characteristics of one community only. Bijjala further adds, "In all my sixty-two years, the only people who have looked me in the eye without a reference to my lowly birth lurking deep in their eyes are the *sharanas*: Basavanna and his men. They treat me as—as what?—(Almost with a sense of wonder) as a human being. Basavanna wants to eradicate the caste structure, wipe it off the face of the earth. Annihilate the varna system. . . . Look at those he has gathered around him: poets, mystics, visionaries. . . . All hard-working people from the common stock. They sit together, indifferent to caste, birth or station." (15)

Treat everyone as 'a human being' only is the argument in *Tale-Danda*. Religion cannot ill-treat anyone, nor can it reduce anyone from his being a human being. We know that greatest evils have been done in the name of God and deadliest wars have been fought in the name of religion. The existence of religion is like that of time. Both have the fluidity and the variance when seen through the human eyes, the eyes that have faith in science, a subject that deals with firm proofs, and Religion, which purely survives in faith. Now, when we know that the principles of science have also changed in certain cases; say for example Newton's gravitational laws have been superseded by Einstein, then Religious beliefs cannot have rigid unalterable sayings. Bijjala explains to his wife Queen Rambhavati the difference between God and a human being and the difference in him and God in the words: "But the one truth I know is that I exist and God doesn't." (15) Now, the question here is: if God doesn't exist, what about the relation or association between God and religion or between man and religion.

Once again Karnad breaks away with the rooted traditional beliefs regarding having a son and regarding birth, caste and creed.

Bijjala: A son is the final goal of human existence! It may be that he drinks your blood and chews your bones to mash. But he is the one who'll keep your soul fed till eternity.

Basavanna: For a *sharana*, physical parentage is of no consequence. A person is born truly only when the guru initiates him into a life of knowledge.

Bijjala: That's what you believe. As a child you tore up your sacred thread and ran away from home. Birth, caste and creed mean nothing to you. (20)

Karnad here disagrees with the established tradition of considering a caste or creed on the strength of "physical parentage." Instead 'Knowledge' is the right canon to judge a human being. In *Chandalika* Tagore presents a similar viewpoint. Ananda, a Buddhist monk, says to a low-caste girl Prakriti, "As I am a human being, so also are you, and all water is clean and holy that cools our heat and satisfies our thirst." (148) The girl reports to her mother: "He said that Janaki bathed in such water as this, at the beginning of her forest exile, and the Guhak, the Chandal drew it for her." (149) We have seen earlier that every rule, be it of science or religion, needs to be reviewed, restructured and deconstructed for better set up and for better strength. Through Manchanna Kramita, a Brahmin who was an adviser to the king, Karnad shows his dissent with the ritual slaughter of animals before the Vedic gods. When fire sacrifices or any other sacrifices are offered to God for religious purposes, it is improper, inhuman, unworthy and beastlike; we cannot justify slaughtering of animals for our own purposes. In Act II, scene v, Madhuvarsa, a *sharana* who is a brahmin by birth, shows his willingness to sacrifice his daughter's life to forward the cause of their great movement. But Basavanna turns down the proposal saying, "No one has a right to sacrifice anyone—not even himself." (39)

In Act II, scene v, we find that Sheelavanta, a cobbler boy, is going to marry Kalavati, a brahmin girl. The author brilliantly develops this delicate matter and handles the situation in a masterly way to achieve new dramatic heights. Here the brahmin girl has no objection in marrying the cobbler boy. But the cobbler boy is hesitant to accept the brahmin girl because the girl "can't stand the smell of leather." (40) King Bijjala, who is a barber by birth, wants to forbid the marriage. Basavanna, a *sharana* saint poet, is not ready for such a kind of wedding because "the orthodox will see . . . mingling of castes as a blow at the very roots of varnashrama dharma." (38) Later he consents for this inter-caste wedding. But the king warns him that it will create an uncontrollable bloodshed. However, the king "staunched the wrath of the people and invited disaster on his own head." (65) The wedding procession also meets a success. Basavanna gives full credit to king Bijjala for this success.

The protection given to *sharanas* proves too costly to the king. His son, Prince Sovideva, conspires against him and imprisons him by bribing Bijjala's own men. Kallappa, who could not be bribed is killed. Basavanna, with his one hundred and fifty thousand *sharanas* fails to save the king. Jagadeva kills king Bijjala in the sanctum. In the words of Damodara: "On the one hand stands the Vedic Dharma, which has branched out in strength over the centuries and now shades the whole of Aryavrata. On the other, there is the *sharana* movement—a pestilence—but of a virulence not seen since the days of Buddha. These two face each other in implacable hostility." (64) Damodar Bhatta, the Queen's priest also states, "civilization has been made possible because our Vedic tradition controls and directs that self-destructive energy. How large-hearted is our dharma! To each person it says you don't have to be anyone but yourself. One's caste is like one's home—meant for one's self and one's family. It is shaped to one's needs, one's comforts, one's tradition. And that is why the Vedic tradition can absorb and accommodate all differences, from Kashmir to Kanya Kumari. And even those said to be its victims have embraced its logic of inequality." (56)

Basavanna knows king Bijjala's help to the *sharanas*. He knows that it was Bijjala's protection to the *sharanas* that made the inter-caste marriage possible. He hopes that "the king will receive his dues from the *sharanas*" (69) because he sings that "He who can turn space into form he alone is a *sharana*." (69) Basavanna, with all his ability and foresight fails to save king Bijjala against Prince Sovideva who wants to make the king and his men pay for defying him at the Treasury. And immediately on the verge of getting powers Sovi declares, "The king is father to his people and the people shall love him and obey him like his offspring. No tongue shall wag against the king or his family or his retinue or his officers. From this moment all *sharanas*, foreigners, and free thinkers are expelled from this land on pain of death. Women and the lower orders shall live within the norms prescribed by our ancient tradition, or else they'll suffer like dogs." (90)

Karnad's *Tale-Danda*, a tragedy, shows Basavanna's "principle of movement and progress in human enterprise"[5] ending in terror and bloodshed. Through conflict and confrontation which go side by side in the drama, Karnad deconstructs the meaning of caste and religion and shows a new community of *sharanas* who condemn idolatry and temple worship, reject anything that is static, believe in equality of sexes and hard work and oppose the caste system.

NOTES

1. A.K. Sinha, "Girish Karnad: Thematic Concerns and Technical Features," p. 54 in this book.
2. M.K. Naik, *A History of Indian English Literature* (New Delhi: Sahitya Akademi, 1982), p. 262.
3. Girish Karnad's preface to *Tale-Danda* (Delhi: Ravi Dayal Publisher, 1993).
4. Rabindranath Tagore, *Three Plays* (Madras: Oxford University Press, 1950), p. 154.
5. Preface to *Tale-Danda*.

Asif Currimbhoy's *The Doldrummers*: The Doldrums of Post-Independence Disillusionment

K. SUNEETHA RANI

Asif Currimbhoy's play *The Doldrummers* depicts the post-Independence disillusionment and disasters as its consequence piquantly. Given the dramatist's interest in observation and presentation of life, the play is very realistic. It stands for a situation where there is no hope, no intention and no future. The characters haunt the readers since the play creates the impression that the play is an episode from our neighbourhood.

This play presents four main characters—Joe, Tony, Rita and Liza. Four characters represent four different categories, of course, not socially and economically, but psychologically. Joe is the only enigmatic character among these. The remaining three speak what they mean and do not pretend as if they are not what they have. Rita and Tony are in love with each other. But each one's love is different in its own sense. For Rita, Tony is the centre of the world. Tony loves to receive gifts, especially from Liza, and in return he can give what the gift presenters expect as women. Liza is a woman who achieves what she wants at any cost.

Rita, unable to bear Tony's swing towards Liza, succumbs to the temptations of Joe and decides to work in the foot-steps of Liza to please Tony with gifts. She invites men who can give her gifts, among whom Joe is also one. Tony for the time being does not mind Rita's activities. Gradually his inner self comes out. After a fight with him, Rita runs towards the sea. Tony runs after her to rescue her but is rescued by her. Rita, pregnant with Joe's child, receives the death news of Joe. Joe disappears physically but his memories, including his child, remain with Rita.

The most striking aspect of the play is symbolism. Here simple things stand for serious facts of life. The dramatist takes the help of symbols to pour his anger and disgust at the contemporary society of postcolonial India. The sound of the waves in the background is sometimes lulling and at other times irritating in its intensity and monotony. This description of the backdrop symbolically stands for the atmosphere pervading in the play. Sometimes the characters find themselves and surroundings pleasant and some other times irritating. Even the sea-breeze is similarly erratic and either blows hard or is terribly still in consonance with tides. Apart from describing the scene, Asif Currimbhoy also gives a picture of the mood in the play which reduces the distance between characters and audience to a great extent.

The kerosene lamp casts shadows on the curtains and the pantomime of life mutely played is seen there, whereas in the play we see life in all its flesh and blood and fully articulated. Both hold a mirror to reality in their own way.

While the three monkeys stand for three different morals, Rita's comparison of themselves with the same stands for complete withdrawal. She says about herself, Joe and Tony, "We three, like blind mice, or better still, like three monkeys, see nothing, hear nothing, do nothing."[1] These three are completely self-indulgent. Unlike the symbols, they refuse to receive anything, not merely evil. They live in watertight compartments where the oxygen is selfishness. They are busy with their self-centred worlds. As Joe rightly puts it, they live in doldrums.

Joe's ring symbolically stands for human relations. He asks Rita to wear it and quickly take it off. Rita does and tells him that there is no need for such gifts since it is no longer a secret and can be done openly by paying cash. Ironically, after Joe s death, his ring reaches Rita mysteriously. Probably the dramatist wanted to establish that however materialistic the world may become, tender sentiments and emotional relations do not completely disappear. Even after his death, Joe's memories and his child remain with Rita to remind her of Joe.

Conversation in the play is no doubt lucid and colloquial. But it is at times absurd without any links. Perhaps it reflects the life-style of the characters. They have no topic to talk about and no issue to discuss and no deep-hearted feelings are seen except in Rita. They talk to kill time and they have no other serious work as well.

There are particular references to the postcolonial, post-Independence Indian scene. Unfortunately or ironically Joe, who criticizes the world, fails to contribute to the world around him or inside him in a positive way. His mind is poisoned by the surroundings and in turn he poisons his surroundings.

Joe presents an Iago-like personality. Distrust of human emotions and relations characterize both the characters. Iago and his personality are extensively interpreted and there are several versions of criticism. Joe is not so enigmatic. His words and behaviour reveal his disgust and disappointment with the world. His character speaks volumes about disillusionment among youth in post-Independence era. The relevance of Satyagraha and the misusing of it is sarcastically expressed by Joe:

> One day we just . . . non-cooperated
> Sat around and merely waited
> Others came and waited too
> Not knowing what; where or who. (3)

Joe, like Iago, does not believe in sentiments and relations. For him love is no different from any other four-lettered word. He describes Tony and Rita as two children with single lollypop. He says about himself, "you put anything to me straight and I see it upside down." (5) He describes himself as:

> I'm the little man with the large pair of scissors. I'm kill-joy and kill-truth put together, and when I can't cut any more, I cut my own nose to spite my face. I'm the public that has no opinion, because I can't bring myself to care a damn. I'm . . . spineless, because it's easier to crawl around that way. Damn you! I'd like to spit in your eye . . . (then weakly) only I don't salivate enough (giggles). (5)

Joe, who comes to us as a misanthrope, himself talks about the dead feelings in human beings. It can be a soul-search or a satire against the world which made him a nihilist. He says, "some things within us also die. For while nothing in the dead can live, something in the living can die." (18)

Cleverly he creates situations to suit his needs. He knows very well when, where and how to strike. Patiently he waits for the right moment to change Rita's attitude towards love and life. He succeeds and benefits. For him there is no difference between love and desire, relations and business. He angrily says: "Love! Respect! Love! Respect! What does it mean? I get sick hearing people talk about it all the time. And what does love have to do with respect anyway. They're the very opposite. You think of the word love like something from a fairy book, patented and germ-free. Like it had to have respectability. Well it's not. It's love that the whore dispenses around the street corner, and it's the most respectable that pay its price." (31) He defends his ideas by giving examples, when Rita accuses calling him crazy, he says: "No more than anybody else Rita. It's just that I get crazier quicker than most. I see how their minds work, and bloat it on a screen. Sure it looks ugly, like little Gulliver noticing the warts on the breasts of the female giants, but it's there. It's large as life, wearing the shackles of the original sin. So why blame me." (29)

Although the characters do not seem to have anything serious to discuss, songs in the play, like Joe's words, explore burning problems. The very first song in Act I scene 2 discusses the question of world peace in an Atomic Age.

Better still let's get shot
Like an as-tro-naut.
Suspended in space
In this doomsday race.

We'll eat atoms for breakfast
Hydrogen for lunch
And when it's time for dinner
We'll chase gals like the old sinner. (33)

The play probably seems to suggest that fight for survival will bring people together and bind them with a zeal for common goal. That is what the freedom struggle did. But after the achievement of Independence, a vacuum was created. There was no noble common aim for which people could fight. Same obsession with the past and disgust and disappointment with the present are echoed in the words of Joe. He compares the flag to a giant tree which started its life as a tender plant. It was the memorial of the martyrs' blood. Identity, Joe says, was found and people were satisfied after Independence. He adds: "But something was still missing. A distortion in the seed. They chose to ignore it, resting on past laurels. Gradually, unknowingly, the tree decayed, the landscape changed into desert, and the fight for survival . . . was inversed. We became monsters. Reptilian. With scales insensitive. With breaths of fire and venomous spittle." (141)

Joe's character raises an important issue. After Independence the future of Indians with foreign blood became a big question: not just their future but their status in society. They were no longer respected and received. Moreover they were treated like outcastes. Joe expresses his agony for this situation. Being a part of the community his survival becomes difficult. This is one of the problems created by colonialism. Joe's agony bursts out in his words: "Since the mirror showed almost everyone the same, they all thought they were the human, and we . . . we . . . the half ones. Those with heads human and bodies like monsters. We . . . we . . . became the still-born ones. Partial monsters all the more horrible because we still retained the basic elements. Was the natural the distortion, or the distortion the natural. Nobody quite knew." (41-42)

Joe represents the section of illegitimate children. The struggle for existence in a society which demands legitimacy above all might have been responsible for the transformation of a philanthropist into a misanthropist. A scholar turned into a cynic is what we see in Joe. "Tony's a natural born boy here. His mother had pangs of childbirth before he was born. He's clean. Not me. I just slithered out with a lot of muck. My Ma never went to the hospital. They didn't take her in, because Pa wasn't around to register her. I just came off in the street. That's why the smell remains." (16)

Joe comes to us not only as a misanthropist but also as a misogynist. He reveals his contempt for women. All women are same for him. They have only one thing in common that describes them that is their female identity. "I'm out, and I want to stay out. Rita or Liza, you're all the same to me. Women with something nice between their legs. No more." (30)

But he also expresses his concern for women suppressed by men. His words remind one of Kamala Das's words about man-woman relationship. Joe says, "Man always pins a woman 'neath him. Like a butterfly, with beautiful wings, spread out and pinned. For a woman, it's crucifixion." (25)

It appears as if Joe is testing human values and relations when he instigates and encourages Rita to take to prostitution and when he gives clue to Tony that Rita is enjoying with other men and leads him to a fight with his rival. He succeeds in his attempts, and his opinion that all these sentiments are illusory is proved once again. He tells Rita,

> We started a game, don't you remember? As long as it was a present, and it came from a friend of Tony, it was mutually acceptable. Tony wouldn't mind . . . you saw for yourself he didn't, right in true face of it. So we started the game with one party, and now I offer myself as another candidate. There's no difference, Rita. It's my right, as much as it is his, as long as we are not Tony. (51-52)

He continues:

> "Et tu Brute?" Et tu Brute! These are not mere words Rita; this is the proof. The proof to all our existence. Love, Hope, Faith. Friendship. It all boils down to one thing alone. Me. Me. That I live, God knows how. That I shall die, that I know. This act of mine is what we all live by. Even you who have failed to realize it yet, will find it so. Wear the ring, Rita. It carried the witchcraft of humanity. But wear it only for a while. It has to be passed on to others, so that everything stillborn may live in its transfiguration. (52)

At some point his intentions are difficult to understand. He expresses disbelief in human relations. He drives Rita to prostitution in the name of love. He presents a ring to Rita as a token of relationship. Does it mean that Joe has fascination and passion for Rita and manipulated everything merely to have sex with her? Or does it mean that he never had belief in human relations and sentiments and wanted to disprove them? If he is so frank and straightforward, why does he present his ring to Rita? If he feels that all human relations are financial and material, why should he take the help of a gift? Obviously, it is not to establish a good impression of himself on Rita. Because, from the beginning, with his comments and interference he forms a very bad impression on Rita. She rightly points out:

> Sometimes I think Joe never existed. That he was only part of you and I. Something evil hidden within us. That it appeared one day as an apparition, and called himself Joe. That his absence does not mean that he has been exorcised, like the devil, because he's already set into motion a train of events . . . and knows where it will end. (59)

He may be a part of characters and not an individual character, which provokes them to take wrong path. Perhaps Joe stands for the deterioration of values and disappointment with life that exist in everyone's heart, especially Rita and Tony. It is not Joe who shows the path to Rita but it is her own suppressed self which comes out and dominates her life.

Joe is compared to 'hand' by Tony and to 'teeth' by Liza. Tony says that Joe was a part of himself. In his absence Tony feels as if he has lost his hand. He compares his experience without Joe to the feelings of a man who tries to use his hand which is separated from him. Liza says that without Joe, Tony and Rita look lonesome like one of the front teeth missing. His presence is a necessary evil. He becomes a part of the small world of Tony and Rita. When he is around, they fight with him and in his absence they miss him.

In this play, Rita seems to be the only character, in whose heart springs up true love. But this love is projected as blind and indiscriminate. She always tries to project Tony as an independent and self-reliant person whereas the truth is completely different. The other two characters know very well about Tony and Tony himself does not have high ideas about himself. But it is Rita who always tries to elevate Tony beyond human beings, place him on a higher pedestal and worship.

She expects same sincerity from Tony like hers for him. Unfortunately, she being the model of sincerity gets transformed into a prostitute to appease the desires of Tony. Joe encourages her to take Tony's model. Before being succumbed to Joe's temptations Rita asks Tony: "Why did you do it Tony? Why did you do it! Isn't my love enough for you? I've given you all of it. Why shouldn't I expect all from you. Woman's no different from a man." (20)

Rita starts hating herself. But at the same time she cannot help loving Tony and keeps trying to please him with gifts. She says, "Like one hates oneself at times, but cannot avoid living with since it forms part of oneself." (66)

Rita returns Joe's ring saying that now that it has become a routine and a business, Joe can pay her in cash. But his child and his ring both remain with Rita even after Joe's death. When asked about the father of her unborn child, Rita says with contempt: "You're back-dated on your news Liza, or don't you know. Visit the 'Circus Inn' sometime and catch up on the gory details. They must be betting there on 'which one dun it.'" (64)

Rita, a sensitive and sincere lover, turns out to be very blunt. It is Tony who is responsible for this. He is a parasite for whom his survival and pleasure are more important than anything else. This very amoral Tony, who thinks that there is nothing wrong in receiving gifts and who fails to oppose his rival's proceedings towards Rita and accepts Rita's affairs with many men for the sake of gifts he receives, says, "You smell of two-dozen kinds of sweat." (62)

Liza, who is described by the playwright as a technicolour doll with everything about her painted, talks sensibly at times smashing the prejudices and inhibitions of the other two—Joe and Rita. Joe always perceives himself as an intellectual who is rejected by the world which is much below his level and so could not understand him. Rita has similar feelings about her love, morality and devotion.

Liza says:

> You know you're all crazy, the three of you, you know it. You're all . . . somewhat schizophrenic as Joe calls it . . . and you know it and can't be bothered even to allow it to change. God almighty, what a smug little world you three have created for yourselves. You look down on others because they all have, as Joe says, hyena like red bottoms and early tops. Well what the hell do you think you have? Turn the mirror upside down sometimes and you'll see yourselves no different. No different, you understand. (39)

Liza is down-to-earth and practical. Throughout the play she gives an impression that she has no sentiments and feelings. But when she comes to know about Rita's pregnancy, she responds in an unusual way saying that as a woman she can understand Rita very well. She confesses that Tony never belonged to her completely, There was something in him which longs for and which belongs to Rita. Her words also throw light on society's influence on her character and life-style. She advises Rita:

> Look Rita, I've got a far more practical solution. Listen to me. I have a friend. He kept reassuring me that I was completely safe with him because he claimed to be a doctor. At first I thought he meant safe the other way . . . you know, a platonic friendship . . . until I found out that he meant otherwise. It turned out he really was a doctor . . . and what's more a practising doctor. He told me if I ever knew anyone in trouble, he could fix her up . . . you know. (64)

The concept of love is interpreted differently by the four characters in the play. For Tony, what matters is gifts. He can distribute his love to any number of people provided he gets what he wants in return. Liza knows how to enjoy life. She can mould people and circumstances according to her needs. She never expresses her love for anybody. Joe is a peculiar character with negative opinions about all human relationships. Rita, who appears to be sensible, fails to discriminate between possessiveness or selfishness and love.

She takes the clue from Joe and after some conflict becomes a doll in the model of Liza. The very term love loses its meaning here.

Fascination for Western life-style and the process of acculturation are meaningfully depicted in the play. The atmosphere in the play is not totally Indian. It is moulded after or rather contaminated by the western concept of self and love. Two young students approach Rita, the call girl, and their conversation unveils the western process of education which teaches everything that is unnecessary before students reaching the stage of discriminating between necessary and unnecessary and before they can realize the boundaries.

The dramatist's concern for cultural infiltration (negative) and psychological slavery of Indians to the imperialists is revealed in Joe's words:

> One day we met a Dharma Bum
> He came from America and called us Chum
> Swore every night he slept with Nirvana
> Smoked a weed he called . . . Mirajuana. (3)

These words are a satire aimed at the hollow terms which function as temporary resorts for the disillusioned and frustrated youth. These are not mere terms but hallucinations which guide the youth towards peril.

Asif Currimbhoy perceives post-Independence India from a different angle, that is from the perspective of Indians with foreign blood. They are Indians facing all the problems that Indians face, but at the same time are looked upon as aliens by their fellow Indians. The play brilliantly presents Indians like Joe, Liza, Tony and Rita surrounded by myriad problems in the postcolonial era. *The Doldrummers* is unique in its theme, characterization, treatment and technique.

NOTE

1. Asif Currimbhoy, *The Doldrummers* (Bombay: Soraya), p. 39.

Cultural Interaction between Marathi and English Poetry: A Study in Translation

P.S. KASTURE

Culture is a way of leading a refined, cultivated life. Man purposefully creates new things, he preserves them and transfers them to the coming generation. Such a life is said to be a refined life. Culture is the activity of thought and receptiveness. Culture includes anything that can be communicated from one generation to another. The culture of the people is the social heritage, a complex whole includes known beliefs, moral laws and customs.

Creation, preservation and transfer of culture is processed through language. The trio, words, sounds and their meaning, with its dual nature of being constant in one sense and ever changing in another, is an influential medium of culture. Literature reflects society and its culture. It not only highlights external appearance, but hints at the peculiar tendencies, instincts, customs of the society. In this process of transfer from generation to generation, culture continually changes. No live culture is static. When two societies come in constant contact with each other, their mutual response leads to cultural interaction between the two. Literature of the time naturally reflects this phenomenon.

Before the British rule, the Mughal emperors ruled India through centuries. Under the influence of Mulla-Maulavis, many Hindus were converted to Islam. Politics and literature about government-administration contained many Urdu and Pharasi words. Aristocratic Hindus indulged in the luxurious life-style of their emperors. Hindu art was also influenced by Mughal art. Such and many other changes took place in India under the Mughal rule. But basically Hindu society, social and cultural life in India showed no great change then. On the other hand, the onslaught of the British on India, their centralised rule throughout India for a century or two left a deep mark on the Indian life. The Indians did not approve of many aspects of this new culture but they were deeply influenced by English literature and sciences.

This is an example of a significant cultural interaction. It is a continual and manifold process as life itself. This paper aims at only one field of cultural interaction, namely, translation. Because of the bitter constraint of length, the corpus of sampling is limited, though it is quite representative of the whole. The paper deals with translations of some modern Marathi poems into English and vice versa.

I

Theoreticians have defined translation in various ways. Very often, if not always, translation has been perceived as an autonomous scholarly activity aimed at the "reproducing" (Nida, 1949-76), "substituting"/"replacement" (Catford, 1965:1 & 20), "transfer" (Brislin, 1976:1), "conversion" (Tweney, 1976:138), "replacement"/"transfer" (Pinchuk, 1977:30 and 35), or "rendering" (Newmark, 1988:5) of the 'message' (Nida), 'text' (Catford), 'thoughts/ideas' (Brislin), 'meaningful utterance' (Tweney), 'words'/'meanings' (Pinchuk), or 'meaning' (Newmark) of one language into/by another language.[1]

Translation is replacement of a text in a Source Language (SL) by an equivalent text in a Target Language (TL), so that such a text fulfills a function in TL equivalent to its function in SL. This is a need based translation generally undertaken by the speakers of TL. Translation can also function as a cross-cultural event in TL, as "an act of communication across cultural barriers."[2] This is undertaken by SL speakers or TL speakers to enlarge mutual understanding of their respective cultural heritage. "Any translation is, in fact, a kind of discovery. Discovery of unknown literature, unknown culture, unknown knowledge."[3]

Translation into English from regional literatures is necessary not only to bridge the gap between India and the West, but also to create a feeling of literary oneness within India. India is a multi-lingual nation. Its language and literature situation is quite complex. Because of the unfamiliarity of many regional languages, literature in those languages remains unfamiliar to many Indian readers. The ideal way is to learn the language of the literature, but practically this is not possible often. So, in a multi-lingual situation, for inter and intra cultural interaction, translation is one widely accepted resort. In the present Indian situation English presents itself as one of the chief languages of translation.

Translation of poetry is the most difficult, if not impossible. Translation takes the form of transcreation here, which cannot invoke the same responses between the users of the SL and TL. Poetry exploits and integrates the resources of the whole language—phonology, morphology, syntax and lexicon. No two languages can be expected to have an equivalent or symmetrical organisation of all these, particularly if they are not cognate languages, for example, Indian regional language like Marathi and English. Absolute anonymity is impossible even within the same language. Establishing equivalence of text-segments between two languages (SL and TL) is doubly impossible, particularly with literary texts in unrelated languages.

Much discussion has been done on the theory and practice of translation, role and function of a translator, various levels of problems faced by a translator. This paper tries to look at the situation/process/ problem not from the point of view of the translator, but that of the TL reader, who is also bilingual like the translator himself and has the same SL.

III

This paper confines itself to the consideration of translation of some modern Marathi poems into English and vice versa. Two famous modern Marathi poets who are the products of the Indian society under the British rule have been selected for discussion viz. Indira Sant and Vinda Karandikar.

Indira Sant's self-engaging cult of mind is congenial to her lyrical poetry. Most of her poems express her deep sense of loss for her dear departed husband. Though her poetic world is limited, one wonders at the richness and depth with which she pursues and captures the various shades of this experience. There is a happy synthesis of inspirations, lyrical instinct and language in her poetry. This is the secret of her success as a poet. This point of her strength in Marathi proves to be the most difficult aspect for a translator, especially when TL is a foreign language like English. Language being an integral part of the poetic whole does not allow its replacement. The cultural gap also presents, at times, an unsurmountable gulf.

In her poem *Padayatra*, "The Pilgrimage,"[4] she talks about tragic human predicament. The path of life offers some moments of happiness, but human life is essentially rigged with some unknown curse. Indira Sant describes natural continuity of human existence, the feet begin to move, no measure how much time, how many paths and how many horizons are left behind: "Tari Pawale chalat rahatat" (62)—"Yet the feet pursue their goal." (63) The Marathi version hints at aimless, directionless wandering away, not purposeful pursuing of a goal as indicated in English translation.

> Chalata Chalata
> Asa ek kshana yeto ki pudhe
> Wata uratach nahi, (62)
> There comes a time
> When no path is seen;

The Marathi version implies non-existence of path but the English connotes inability of the traveller to find it. Non-existence of path leaves man with no hope, but to confront "anant bhishan asa awakash" (62)—terrible, endless space, not 'future.' The English version connotes not the engulfing and encircling emptiness but promising coming time. This situation forces on man the acceptance of the awareness of mortality as a condition of human existence.

> Aani paya khalachi muthabhar mati ghatta
> Dharun thevayachi asate—tyach mutheet (62)
> Take possession of your faith,
> Hold on to it tightly. (63)

'Faith' in English translation fails to be exact. So the pathetic intensity in the Marathi version is lost.

Even the note (79) with literal meaning does not enlighten reader any further. Awareness of mortality is not conveyed on conceptual level but is a forced personal experience. "Paya khalchi muthahar *mati . . . tyach mutheet.*" (62, italics mine)

Apparently one may feel that such problems may be avoided if the poet himself does the work of translation. A translator often tends to be too literal and loses the general drift. If a poet tries it himself, he may make a few changes to render the meaning in a better and clearer manner. But Vinda Karandikar's translation of his own Marathi poems proves that this belief is not always true. Vinda Karandikar (G.V. Karandikar) is one of the most famous experimentalist poets in modern Marathi poetry. He tries to change poetic language, metre, style and construction for conveying his complex awareness. In his poetry one perceives a mature mind enriching itself with new thoughts, faiths and experiences of life.

Vinda's 'abhanges' in the original have in the title 'Desperate or Aggressive' as a qualifying word. He speaks of the contemporary reality but exploits the devotional tradition through allusions, distortions and verbal associations, thus bringing the past and the present, the East the West in a sharp confrontation. (112-13)

> Deityanche ya bhaya Bhaya Devanchehi;
> Bhaya yachi dehi yachi dola (38)
> I fear the devils the gods too I fear;
> Fear's Beatific vision is here as I live. (39)

The poet's 'Beatific Vision' of fear fails to recreate the emotional equivalence in English due to the loss of native cultural reference. "Literal translation would be 'fear, while the body exists and the eyes see'; but the mode of diction in the original is suggestive of the devotional poetry of the saints which asserts the direct and sensuous apprehension of the Deity." (113) This note by the poet highlights the awareness of his limitations as a translator. Only a poem, original or translated, which is a complete whole in itself, can lay a claim to creativity.

In his poems like 'The Insane,' Vinda tries to create symbols through narrative forms.

> Apalya gharatale matiche madke
> Manamurad phodun ti dehantachya yatrela nighalee (102)
> The earthen pitcher at home
> She smashed pleasurably and started on a body-ending pilgrimage. (103)

In the notes Vinda explains that the poet sees in this insane woman, the symbol of the life of a creative artist. (118) 'Earthen pitcher' fails to translate the Hindu concept of representing human body as 'madke' and the Hindu ritual to carry fire in 'madke' to cemetery and break it at the last rite. Breaking of the form liberates the soul. If translation is an attempt to recreate similar responses in TL as in SL, then such a loss of the essential cultural ethos in the translated version, perhaps, indicates the area of untranslatability. Of course, every attempt at translation from Marathi to English, is not necessarily a failure. In spite of cultural differences, at times, the translator is able to recreate meaningful equivalences in TL. For example, Indira Sant's 'Snake-Skin' (Kata) and Vinda's 'Grace' (krupa).

IV

T.V. SarDeshmukh's translation of Emily Dickinson's poems from English to Marathi exemplifies the other side of the issue. Fortunately, SarDeshmukh's translation successfully presents Emily Dickinson with her full force. This translation is not merely a replica of the American version, but an artistic whole in its own capacity of being creative.

Emily Dickinson does not talk of her experiences in a loud tone. Her words are measured gently and delicately. Nature is lovingly associated with her inner life and hence is often present in her poetry through various images. Love, death, bereavement, dejection, immortality and eternity are some of her favourite subjects. The tenderness and intensity of her feelings is felt everywhere.

While experiencing the surging of love, consequent purging of despair and flowering of mind, Emily Dickinson must also have felt distancing of love. This dual experience harshly cuts the essence of life and creativity. This is death to her; then continue a joyless life under an eclipse. One who loves confronts such moments with varying degrees of intensity. Dickinson's love for life is counter-balanced by her unbelieving fascination for death. Love is a bridge between life and death. Dickinson talks to her lover with delicate courtesy. In this tenderness she weaves the fidelity of her mind and her life-values in such a way that her tenderness shines like the blade of a sword. Her loneliness is not miserable but magnanimous. She bids a courageous farewell to her hopes of happiness and accepts mutely all forms of sorrow. The translator is able to recreate Dickinson's mood and rhythm in equally chiselled language by creating artistic equivalences like 'Sacrament'—(krupa)

> Where Thou art—that is Home—
> Cashmere—or Calvary—the same—
> . . . . What Thou dost—is Delight—
> Bondage as Play—be sweet—
> Imprisonment—Content—
> And Sentence—Sacrament—
> Just We two—meet.
> Tu asasghila tithe maza ghar re
> maga te kashmir aso ki calvary!
> . . . . Tu karasheel tyata maza ananda
> Bandhan hu krida
> Keideta samadhana
> Shiksheta krupa
> fakta tu-me bhetayala hava! (29)[7]

The last line constitutes the paradox of fate. Where the meeting of 'We two' is doubtful, happy dialogue is an impossibility and sorrow an inevitable presence. Happiness how dejecting, and suffering how painful, but Emily Dickinson talks of it so simply and so naturally:

> If certain, when this life was out—
> That yours and mine, should be

I'd toss it yonder, like a Rind,
And take Eternity. (511)
Ya jivananatee
tu-me eikatra yeu:
tar bathi phekun dyavi
tasa he jiwit udavun dile asate
aani anantata chakhali asati me. (31)

One wonders how Emily Dickinson must have driven to bear such a hopeless future in the present with so grand a balance! The translator is able to render the very spirits of Emily Dickinson and present the experience originally in Marathi with exactness and directness. His creation of native Marathi images like 'gundali' to wind the months in balls or 'Bathi' for 'Rind,' 'chakhana' for 'take' points to the success of translation as recreation.

V

In the present linguistic complex in India, English presents itself as a link language/medium. So translation into English from regional languages like Marathi definitely serves the purpose and so is a significant cultural activity. However, the translatory problems faced not only by a translator but also by a bilingual reader make us think about the targeted reader. A remark of the translators of Indira Sant's poems raises one basic question. "In this book are Indira Sant's poems, speaking in English on behalf of the originals to the English-speaking reader for his pleasure and instruction." (18) If such translation is meant primarily for an English-speaking reader not with Marathi as his mother tongue, a sincere translator, in spite of the inherent drawbacks, surely widens his horizon. A bilingual reader, with English as SL/TL and his mother tongue (Marathi) as TL/SL perceives such lapses in the translations but also apprehends their naturalness in the process of translation. Content and expression together create a work of art. To replace only the linguistic part of it, and that too in a foreign tongue naturally puts severe constraints on a translator. Even the poet himself, after creating a poem in one language (e.g. Marathi), is not always successful in recreating it in English. The difficulty is not with his proficiency in English. He can create a new artistic whole in English for regional concepts/modes. The difference in the cultural ethos between the East and the West contributes significantly to this linguistic transfer. On the other hand, an eminent Indian poet like Nissim Ezekiel, who directly writes in English, faces no such problem as he discovers proper expression for his experience in the very process of creation.

But the situation changes, though not from the reader's point of view, but that of the translator, when he deals with English as SL and a regional Indian language (e.g. Marathi) as TL. His long association with English helps his perception. Marathi being his mother tongue is a powerful TL in his hand. Though the element of cultural untranslatability cannot be totally eliminated, it can be successfully managed. Perception of SL and creation in TL is the index of his success. Such a translation proves to be an artistic recreation of the original. This is one of the ideal situations for cultural interaction.

NOTES

1. B.R. Bapuji, "Social Meaning of Translation in Modern Times," cyclostyled lecture notes, Third Refresher Course in Linguistics, University of Hyderabad, March 1993, p. 1.
2. Bh. Krishnamurti, "A Set of Postulates on Translation—Theory and Practice," Inaugural Address, Third Refresher Course, p. 1.
3. P.R. Dadegaonkar, "New Lamps for the Old: An Inquiry into translation Process, " in *Calts Working Papers*, vol. I, Jan. 1990, p. 73.
4. *Snake-Skin and Other Poems of Indira Sant*, trans. Vrinda Nabar and Nissim Ezekiel (Bombay: Nirmala Sadananda, 1975), pp. 62-63.
5. *Poems of Vinda*, trans. G.V. Karandikar (Bombay: Nirmala Sadananda, 1975), pp. 112-13.
6. *The Complete Poems of Emily Dickinson,* ed. Thomas H. Johnson (Boston: Little, 1960; Indian rpt. Delhi: Kalyani).
7. T.V. SarDeshmukh, "Emilychya Anganat, " *Stree*, March 1977.

Viewing Love through Wit: Structure of Three Post-Independence Poems

PRAFULLA K. JAGADEB

Post-Independence Indian English poetry differs from pre-Independence poetry not only in its themes, but also in its structure. Generally speaking, the structure of most pre-Independence Indian English poems depended on a simple, linear development of the poet's thoughts and feelings, and images were often chosen from traditionally poetic sources, such as nature and folklore.

But Independence changed all that, and many of the important post-Independence poets adopted a different attitude, necessitating the use of wit. The reasons were two-fold. First, after the attainment of Independence, the poets did not need to be patriotic or nationalistic or even 'romantic.' On the other hand, they found national life expanding in many directions, "with great variety and complexity." As free citizens of a free country, they tried to bring under the ambit of their poetry all that great change. In other words, they could not close their eyes to unsavoury aspects of social or individual experiences and concentrate only on its 'romantic' side.

Most of the post-Independence Indian English poets wrote a type of poetry which immediately distinguished them from their counterparts in the pre-Independence era, and the unifying and comprehensive nature of which can be compared to what Cleanth Brooks called "the poetry of wit." Defining this poetry of wit, Brooks says: "Wit is not merely an acute perception of analogies; it is a lively awareness of the fact that the obvious attitude toward a given situation is not the only possible attitude . . . the only poetry which possesses high seriousness in the deepest sense is the poetry of wit."

T.S. Eliot, too, makes the two-fold description of wit in his celebrated discussion of English metaphysical poets; the first kind as constant "amalgamation of disparate experience" with its highly peculiar "alliance of levity and seriousness," and the second variety as a "tough reasonableness beneath the slight lyric grace." Reference may also be made to Richards's description of the poetry of inclusion and stable poise in his well-known essay "The Imagination": "Compared with him [the poet] the ordinary man suppresses nine-tenths of his impulses, because he is incapable of managing them without confusion. He goes about in blinkers because what he would otherwise see would upset him. But the poet through his superior power of ordering experience is freed from this necessity. Impulses which commonly interfere with one another and are conflicting, independent, and mutually distractive, in him combine into a stable poise."

Because of its all-inclusive nature, "the poetry of wit" appears to cut across a greater variety of experiences than perhaps any other kind of poetry. It is structured through its concomitants like irony, paradox, ambiguity, conceit or integrated organic images or metaphors. Because of the necessity to treat new theme under the changed conditions after Independence, Indian English poets of the said period took recourse to wit; how well they wielded it would be the subject of our study which follows.

Of the pre-Independence Indian English poets, Sarojini Naidu's pre-occupation with the theme of love was most consistent. Her volume *The Sceptred Flute* contains many such poems including a long one, "The Temple" which has sections. It would be revealing to compare her poems on love with similar poems written by poets after Independence, particularly in respect of their structure. For example the poem "To Love" in the section "Songs of Life and Death" is built on the theme that the beloved does not deny Love anything:

> O Love! of all the riches that are mine,
> What gift have I withheld before thy shrine?
>
> What tender ecstasy of prayer and praise

Or lyric flower of my impassioned days?
What poignant dream have I denied to thee
Of secret hope, desire, and memory;

Or intimate anguish of sad years, long dead.
Old griefs unstaunched, old fears uncomforted?

What radiant prophecies that thrill and throng
The unborn years with swift delight of song?

O Love! of all the treasures that I own,
What gift have I withheld before thy throne.

The feelings expressed in this poem are simple and direct, without any complexities of wit or ambiguity or even secret or devious desires. What distinguishes the poem is not so much the so-called "riches" provided, but the simple, personal involvement with the riches such as "tender ecstasy," "poignant dream," "intimate anguish," and "radiant prophecies." These suggest the poetic direction, establish the rhetorical content, and on the whole, make the poem a simple, emotional expression of love.

Another love poem of Sarojini Naidu is "Sorrow of Love":

Why did you turn your face away?
Was it for grief or fear
Your strength would fail or your pride grow weak
If you touched my hand, if you heard me speak;
After a life-long year?

Why did you turn your face away?
Was it for love or hate?
or the spell of the wild miraculous hour
That hurled our souls with relentless power
In the eddying fires of fate?

Turn not your face from me. O love!
Shall sorrow of Death conspire
To set our suffering spirits free
From the passionate bondage of Memory
Or the thrall of the old desire.

The structure of this poem is linear and the feelings expressed are simple, though the rhetorical-emotional content is better realized than in the earlier one. There is direct personal communion ("If you touched my hand, if you heard me speak") as well as a tone of personal reflectiveness ("That hurled . . . /eddying fires of fate"). The poem remains a simple, though intense, expression of love.

While the structure of Sarojini Naidu's love poems contains different moods, the structure remains basically simple and linear, and depends on the working-out of one particular emotion in relation to love. We may recall Richards speaking of two different ways to organize impulses and emotions in poetry: "There are two ways in which impulses may be organised: by exclusion and by inclusion, by synthesis and by elimination. . . . A poem of the first group is built out of sets of impulses which run parallel, which have the same direction. In a poem of the second group the most obvious feature is the extraordinary heterogeneity of the distinguishable impulses."

If Sarojini Naidu's poems on love analyzed above belong to the first group, the love poems of Nissim Ezekiel and Shiv Kumar belong to the second group, as categorized by Richards. Ezekiel and Shiv Kumar are free from Sarojini Naidu's romantic subjectivism even when they treat such a personal emotion as love. This is because Ezekiel and Kumar are able to carry on "proper criticism" and inspection of their experiences that taught them to recognize the presence of heterogeneous, sometimes opposed, feelings and emotions. Instead of being outpourings of linear emotional outburst, their poems are linked to the elements of irony, ambiguity, paradox and other qualities we usually associate with "wit" or a witty treatment of experience. For example, in Ezekiel's poem "Love Sonnet," the surroundings—the cafe, the hill, the birds and the city lights—get linked with the poet's emotions which are "turbulent" and "passionate," only to be metamorphosed into a lightness ("floating down the hill, as on a cloud"), finally to disintegrate into a "certain happiness" which is like death ("to die"):

> This cafe, on the hill among the birds,
> Could house a passing cloud.
>   The city's lights

Are coming on.
You and I wait for words;
Our love has formed like dew in summer nights.
The wind has ruffled up your hair:
We look in consort at the distant sea,
And feel it turbulent and salty there,
A passionate and perpetual mystery.
Floating down the hill, as on a cloud,
Proud as lovers are, inarticulate.
We lose ourselves in mingling with the crowd,
Not unafraid of this ambiguous fate.
We look inquiringly at road and sky,
A certain happiness would be—to die.

The setting of the poem is a cafe on the hill in the evening. But there is no one-directional outpouring of a particular kind of emotion, to the exclusion of all other emotions, as in the two poems of Sarojini Naidu analyzed above. Their feelings and impulses, on the other hand, have been organized, as Richards would say, not "by exclusion," but "by inclusion." In other words, as lovers they recognise that a bunch of heterogeneous feelings are reflected by some of the richly ambiguous images used by the poem. Regarding the birth of their love, the speaker says, "our love has formed like dew on summer nights." This "dew" image suggests not only the spontaneity and naturalness of their love; it also serves to hint at the fragility, the vulnerability of their love as also its precarious proximity to death; anytime it might evaporate into thin air. Similarly, when the speaker says that they "look at the distant sea/and feel it turbulent and salty there/A passionate and perpetual mystery," the epithets 'turbulent' and a 'passionate and perpetual mystery' appear to describe their love as much as they describe the sea. The next two images also mirror their feelings as lovers. Their feeling of light-hearted, carefree elation has been captured by the line "floating down the hill, as on a cloud." And they walk down the hill, from the cafe, without any exchange of words, "proud as lovers, inarticulate." The feelings regarding the fragile, "turbulent" and mysterious nature of love come back, leading to inarticulations. Again, when they "lose" themselves "in mingling with the crowd," forgetting their special identity as lovers, it may also be a realization that many in the crowd might also have been lovers and victims of the same feelings: They are no more afraid of their strength and courage from the "crowd," looking inquiringly at "road and sky," wondering what their path as lovers might have in store for them. Thus, one may say, the simultaneous presence of a heterogeneity of feelings as a lover, has given to the poem its peculiar charm.

In Shiv Kumar's poem "Walking on Ice," love is linked with "treacherous ice," "fluffy snow" and "truncated boulders" to end finally in the "cracked crust of/partially thawed ice," and "slush":

Loving you
is like walking warily on treacherous ice,
filed craftily into one continuous
sheet of Belgian glass,
between truncated boulders
of fluffy snow,
so that each time I slip
I imagine myself
exposed to your derisive laughter.
Won't you relent a little
so that I could plant my heels
into the cracked crust of
partially thawed ice?
Even slush is safer to wade through.

While discussing the features of metaphysical poetry of seventeenth century England, Helen Gardner defines conceit thus: "A conceit is a comparison whose ingenuity is more striking than its justness, or, at least, is more immediately striking. All comparisons discover likeness in things unlike: a comparison becomes a conceit when we are made to concede likeness while being strongly conscious of unlikeness." Kumar's comparison of loving his beloved with "walking warily on ice" admirably fits Helen Gardner's definition of a conceit. The unlikeness of the comparison is self-evident, for the thought of a piece of 'ice' is in direct contrast to the conventional ideas regarding the "warmth" of love. But the "ingenuity" of Kumar's comparison is finally convincing by the poetic flash it is capable of generating in the mind of the reader. Kumar's elaboration of the comparison makes the conceit an expanded one, and the carefully-worked-out comparison aptly brings out the precarious nature of his love, particularly when we are told that the lady is used to expose the speaker to her "derisive laughter." The image of 'slush' in the last line of the poem hammers home the precariousness of the 'love-walk' that the speaker has chosen to indulge in to get the love of his mistress. The extended conceit has a sharp visual quality, and the details like "one continuous/sheet of Belgian glass," "truncated boulders/of fluffy snow" emphasize the amount of care and caution necessary for winning the so-called love of the beloved. The poet's prayer ("won't you relent a little") continues the ice-conceit, insofar as the speaker prays for secure and firm walk on the path of love, to "plant" his heels "into the cracked crust of/partially thawed ice." The speaker is aware of the object position he has been reduced to, because of his irresistible love for the lady. But his witty attitude to his position saves him from indulging in the kind of self-mockery that many "romantic" lovers seem to inflict on the reader when put into such a condition.

If Kumar's poem "Walking on Ice" is structured through conceits, the structure of Kamala Das's poem "The Looking Glass" is built by startlingly new, unconventional and apparently unpoetic images:

> Getting a man to love you is easy
> Only be honest about your wants as
> Woman. Stand nude before the glass with him
> So that he sees himself the stronger one
> And believes it so, and you so much more
> Softer, younger, lovelier. . . . Admit your
> Admiration. Notice the perfection
> Of his limbs, his eyes reddening under
> The shower, the shy walk across the bathroom floor,
> Dropping towels, and the jerky way he
> Urinates. All the fond details that make
> Him male and your only man. Gift him all.

Gift him what makes you woman, the scent of
Long hair, the musk of sweat between the breasts,
The warm shock of menstrual blood, and all your
Endless female hungers, oh yes, getting
A man to love is easy, but living
Without him afterwards may have to be
Faced. A living without life when you move
Around, meeting strangers, with your eyes that
Give up their search, with ears that hear only
His last voice calling out your name and your
Body which once under his touch had gleamed
Like burnished brass, now drab and destitute.

The poem has for its theme the secrets necessary for winning a man's love and the despairing condition of "living/without him." Looked at in this way, the poem has two 'movements': the first sixteen lines give us the "secrets" and the last nine lines the difficult life to be led by the beloved without him. Since the first movement posits that "Getting a man to love you is easy," the secrets are two-fold: first, "only be honest about your wants as/woman" and second, "Gift him all,/Gift him what makes you woman." The first "secret" is then expressed through very startlingly unconventional (so far as an Indian woman's traditional sense of modesty is concerned) and traditionally unpoetic images. These images are mostly visual—the image of the beloved standing "nude before the glass with him," the image of the lover's action ("the shy walk across the bathroom floor/Dropping the towels, and the jerky way he/Urinates.") But the "gifts" that the beloved has to make to the lover are expressed in images of smell and touch—"the scent of/Long hair," "the musk of sweat between the breasts," "The warm shock of menstrual blood." The newness and unconventionality of these images as also their apparently unpoetic nature will be driven when we contrast them with Sarojini Naidu's poem "To Love" in which she also speaks of the "gifts" she has made before the "shrine" of love: "tender ecstasy of prayer and praise," the "lyric flower" of her "impassioned days," the "poignant dream" of her "secret hope, desire and memory," "the intimate anguish of sad years, long dead," etc. These are mainly undefined rhetorical gifts when compared to the bold, unconventional physicalities of Kamala Das's "the musk of sweat between the breasts" and "the warm shock of menstrual blood." Kamala Das's gifts are not only bold but also startlingly 'unwomanly,' almost one may say, unpoetic, unpleasant details best avoided in poetry. But when we remember that details are not poetic *per se* and that no details can be said to be inherently poetic, we see that Kamala Das's details are poetic in the only way they should be poetic, that is, they function integrally in the poem inasmuch as they express for us a lovelorn woman's eager gifts to her lover, a woman who is prepared to give to her lover, in an uninhibited manner, whatever she has to give.

When the beloved faces the difficult condition of living without the lover, Kamala Das calls it "living without life." The beloved's body "which once under his touch had gleamed/Like burnished brass" is now "drab and destitute" because the lover is not there to make proper use of her body. The comparison of the body to "brass" is unusual in Indian English poetry, because traditionally body is compared with a temple or a flower or some other object of nature.

From the foregoing discussion it is clear that the structure of a post-Independence Indian English poem is basically different from that of a pre-Independence Indian English poem because of an integral change in the attitude and perception of the respective poets.

Myopic World and Anchorage of Values

S.T. KAPADIA and T.J. PURANI

> Pedagogy gave up the training of character and devoted itself to equipping the unmoral intellect with all the armoury of science.
>
> Will Durant

Whenever a society enters a new phase of evolution, it inevitably finds itself in throes of a crisis. With the mind-boggling changes taking place today, a creeping fear persists that these changes will, undoubtedly, lead to jettisoning of certain values and ethical code which a civilized society holds clear and which, all agree, form its bedrock. These values are being swept under the carpet and we are daily bombarded with a barrage of new 'values' through the mass media. Aldous Huxely, not long ago, spoke of the dangers of our being subconsciously indoctrinated by our television masters, not only on promoting sales, but also in inducing attitudes of mind.

It does not require any research to know that there has been a perceptible change in the climate and a steady decline of values in practically all the spheres of activities, but more worrisome is what is happening in the field of education since it is a cradle where future citizens are born and nourished, an evil where they are shaped and crucible where they are tested and honed to render them fit to face, what Lalbraith calls, uncertain future. Education is the field which is the theatre and instrument of development, of individual and communal growth and fulfilment. But with education showing signs of palsy one discerns an air of despair and despondency, of disillusionment and disenchantment.

Philosopher McIntyre said that we may be raising a generation of 'moral stutterers.' Some call it moral illiteracy. Educationist Michael Josephson bemoans the present scenario and says that "There is a hole in the moral ozone." Cheating in the examination, bribing teachers, resorting to foul means to make the grade, utter insensitivity to fellow students, bright, unbridled selfishness, lack of respect for others, rude manners, impudent behaviour, tendency to be violent, hatred for those lower in hierarchy . . . the list seems endless! These are the symptoms manifesting themselves in a routine manner. What does one do in such an environment which is hostile to all that is good, moral and ethical. Shall we repeat what Shakespeare said:

> I alone beweep my outcast state.
> And trouble deaf heaven with my bottomless cries,
> And look upon myself and care my fate.

Students in the contemporary world, steeped in the values fostered by the present-day milieu of hardsell, may find the very idea of learning or discussing about moral values to be anachronistic or an 'archaic illusion.' It is not the argument here that we teach the present lot of student the history of ethics and morality as practised down the ages; also we must not, at the same time, simply dispense facts and information produced by the information technology but our responsibility as teachers and educators, in the words of educationist Christina Sommers, goes beyond "Purveying information about the leading ethical theories and developing dialectical skills."

Moral or value education should have as its explicit aim the moral betterment of students and that includes telling them what is right and what is wrong, besides setting an example. "The only means of realizing what is good," says Durant, "is to teach it by education and propagate it by example." Character education is the need of the hour and it is futile to tell students to find and imbibe these values themselves. It is like asking someone in a discovery of truth himself! We cry hoarse over violation of human rights, violence, cruelty, sadism, moral turpitude, defiance to authority and a general disregard for all that this is decent but do we talk about them, obliquely or directly at times, in our class-rooms? Or do we set role models for emulation? As Charles Stuart observes: "Our greatest deformities are within and we must become the severest critics and first reformers of our own soul." "Restoration of values should not be the exclusive pressure of philosophers, thinkers and social reformers, the onus as much rests on teachers as much as on others of the ilk. The teacher must act as bulwork and must not allow education in general and students in particular to surrender before the dominant force which may, in foreseeable future, subvert the entire order of a civilized society and undermine the foundation of the said edifice. If, as a writer puts it, industries and commerce are allowed to colonize pedagogical spheres, then the role of the institutions of learning building a livable society will be in jeopardy. Today the spectacle one witnesses in large number of educational institutions remind us of what one reads in the novel, 'To sir, with love' and the portents are ominous. The current trend of teaching social issues, subjects and topics 'relevant' to market situation and the emphasis on 'progressive teaching methods' has led to the present decline and degeneration. The roots of the malaise have been traced to these progressive methods and teaching and learning of relevant topics by Mr. Christopher Woodhead, Chief Inspector of Schools, U.K., and he bemoans the fact that the whole idea of an enlightened society has received a severe knock. The unwholesome love for so-called 'progressive education' has left pupils floundering in an ethical and cultural vacuum. The desire to teach relevant concerns has led to construction of curricula which leave children confused and unfamiliar with the social canon, and disinheriting them by failing to equip them with enough knowledge of values to enable them to participate in their own culture and the culture of the other communities with which they have to interact. Is it not ironical that on the one hand we talk of the world becoming a global village and on the other the future citizens develop a narrow, parochial, narcissist, violent, sadistic attitude? The words of Ivan Illich ring a bell: "Education becomes unworldly and the world becomes uneducational." The most important lesson is that a nation cannot endure by abandoning excellence or values and treating 'inheritance of values' an impediment to future development. Let the teachers realize that if, as a poet has said, "Utopias are allowed to die," fascist force and fascist mentality will rear their ugly head—they have already—and threaten the existence of a sane society and it's a matter not to rejoice about.

With parents' expectations soaring high, with society and market forces and media determining goals which can be termed unrealistic if not unwholesome, there is the rat race in which fair is foul and foul fair. No one wants to lose the race, and one must not because it has been dinned into our ears that losing or defeat means the end of the world.

The way out is to reinforce values such as decency in public and private life, being honest, helping others, unselfishness, kindness, consideration for others and other virtues through personal example through re-educating parents, through pointing to examples, manifesting such qualities and virtues existing in the society around us and through a kind of moral code which would inculcate the values, qualities and virtues which hold the society together. In the words of Christina Sommers: "I am suggesting that teachers must help children become acquainted with their moral heritage in literature, in religion and in philosophy. I am suggesting that virtue can be taught and that effective moral education appeals to the emotions as well as to the mind. The best moral teaching inspires students by making them keenly aware that their own character is at stake." The 'myopic world' of today needs desperately the anchorage of values and we should not delay further lest the juggernaut of market forces overwhelms us all.